COUNTRY
LORE AND
LEGENDS

Jennifer
Westwood
and
Jacqueline
Simpson

English 🐧 Journeys

PENGUIN BOOKS

Published by the Penguin Group
Penguin Books Ltd, 80 Strand, London WC2R ORL, England
Penguin Group (USA) Inc., 375 Hudson Street, New York, New York 10014, USA
Penguin Group (Canada), 90 Eglinton Avenue East, Suite 700, Toronto, Ontario, Canada M4P 2Y3
(a division of Pearson Penguin Canada Inc.)
Penguin Ireland, 25 St Stephen's Green, Dublin 2, Ireland
(a division of Penguin Books Ltd)
Penguin Group (Australia), 250 Camberwell Road, Camberwell, Victoria 3124, Australia
(a division of Pearson Australia Group Pty Ltd)
Penguin Books India Pvt Ltd, 11 Community Centre, Panchsheel Park, New Delhi – 110 017, India
Penguin Group (NZ), 67 Apollo Drive, Rosedale, North Shore 0632, New Zealand
(a division of Pearson New Zealand Ltd)
Penguin Books (South Africa) (Pty) Ltd, 24 Sturdee Avenue, Rosebank, Johannesburg 2196, South Africa

Penguin Books Ltd, Registered Offices: 80 Strand, London WC2R ORL, England

www.penguin.com

This selection from *Lore of the Land* first published by Penguin 2005
Published in Penguin Books 2009

3

Copyright © Jennifer Westwood and Jacqueline Simpson, 2005
All rights reserved

Set by Rowland Phototypesetting Ltd, Bury St Edmunds, Suffolk
Printed in England by Clays Ltd, St Ives plc

978-0-141-19104-1

www.greenpenguin.co.uk

Penguin Books is committed to a sustainable future
for our business, our readers and our planet.
The book in your hands is made from paper
certified by the Forest Stewardship Council.

PENGUIN BOOKS — ENGLISH JOURNEYS

Country Lore and Legends

Contents

Becket's Murderers

Though no one was tried and executed for it, the murder of Thomas à Becket, Archbishop of Canterbury, did not go unavenged. His death in 1170 in his own cathedral had repercussions in both pious legend and local folk tradition. Some of the most dramatic stories concern Becket's murderers: Reginald Fitzurse, William de Tracy, Richard Lebret, and Hugh de Moreville.

Slayers of clergy could be tried only in ecclesiastical courts, so the only penalty that could be imposed on the four knights was excommunication. This was done on 25 March 1171, but seems to have had little impact on their careers. Within two years of the murder, the four were resident at court, and four years afterwards de Tracy is mentioned as Justiciary in Normandy, a post he held until 1176.

People were not satisfied with this outcome, however, and expressed their discontent by rewriting history. Perhaps, too, they had little idea of what actually happened, which left them free to devise wished-for endings to the story. Consequently, in both early chronicles and later folklore, the murderers were transformed into outlaws, shunned by men and cursed by God.

They supposedly spent the night following the murder at Saltwood Castle, Kent, riding on next day to South Malling, near Lewes, a manor belonging to the see of

Canterbury. Entering, they threw their arms and saddles on the archbishop's dining table, which was standing in the hall. After supper, when they were gathered round the fire, the huge table suddenly shook itself violently and hurled everything to the floor. The heap of belongings was put back, but an hour later the table shook it off again. Soldiers and servants carrying lights searched in vain under the hitherto immoveable table for a cause. Finally, one of the knights told the servants to remove their gear, as the very table deemed it a shameful burden. (As late as the fourteenth century, this table was still shown in the same place, and Borenius in 1932 writes, 'I understand that a table, said to be this very table, is now shown in Lewes museum.')

From South Malling, the knights allegedly rode to Knaresborough Castle in Yorkshire. Local tradition in the nineteenth century pointed out the hall to which they fled and a vaulted prison where they were subsequently confined. After a year, they fled into Scotland, but were very coldly received.

Next they are supposed to have undertaken a penitential journey to Rome. According to one medieval manuscript, William de Tracy went first and he is in fact the only one whose visit there, in 1172, can be documented. The Pope, Alexander III, decreed that they should expiate their sins fighting pagans in the Holy Land. Two went immediately; two followed later. Other accounts have them go straight to the Holy Land – Matthew Paris (c.1200–59) says Henry himself ordered them to go and that they went clad in wool and barefoot.

De Tracy alone, it was said, never fulfilled his vow.

Indeed, according to one medieval report, he never left England. On the other hand, Herbert of Bosham, who wrote a biography of Becket between 1184 and 1187, says that he put off going to Jerusalem and died in agony at Cosenza in Sicily. In truth, what seems to have happened is that he attempted a pilgrimage to the Holy Land, but stayed for a time at the monastery of St Euphemia in Calabria. He was evidently ill and expecting to die, because he made a grant of his Devonshire manor of Doccomb to Christ Church Canterbury for the support of a monk to say masses for the dead. He recovered, however, and returned to England.

De Tracy's hesitations and delays were accounted for differently in popular legend. Because of a belief that he was *primus percussor* (the man who struck the first blow), though the historical evidence indicates Fitzurse, he was said to have been prevented from ever reaching the Holy Land by the 'Tracy Curse'. In his *Worthies of England* (1662), Thomas Fuller explains that, according to 'fond and false tradition', 'it is imposed on Tracys for miraculous penance, that whether they go by land or by water, the wind is ever in their faces'.

The proverbial saying 'The Tracys have always the wind in their faces', meaning roughly that nothing goes right for a Tracy, was, says Fuller, 'disproved by daily experience', as there were two Gloucestershire families descended from de Tracy flourishing in the county in his day.

Though one at least of the knights reached a ripe old age – de Morville lived until 1199 – there seems to have been an almost universal belief that all four died within three or four years of the murder. Their last days are depicted by monastic historians as miserable: people avoided them, no one would eat or drink with them, and the very dogs refused to eat the scraps from their tables. One was even rumoured to have gone mad and murdered his own son.

According to some English chroniclers, they all died after three years' penance in the Holy Land and were buried there. Other sources have them disperse and die in different places. Continental tradition said that they were buried in Flanders; British tradition that it was in the West Country, on the island of Flat Holm, or at Mortehoe, Devon, that at least three of them ended their days.

Bells

Church bells were central to communal life. They rang for weddings, deaths, and funerals; for national and local celebrations; to announce the times of services; and in some places as a sunset curfew. It was a Catholic custom to name and bless a bell before it was hung; this was referred to as its 'baptism'. Another medieval belief was that the sound of church bells drove away the devils of the air, and thunderstorms. In some later tales, fairies regretfully leave a district because church bells make life intolerable for them, as at Inkberrow, Worcestershire.

A recurrent theme concerns the theft or accidental loss of a church bell, which falls into deep water and remains there for ever. A fine example is the tale of the 'Kentsham Bell', told in 1882 to the folklorist Charlotte Burne by a Herefordshire woman whose father had learned it years before from his nurse (the place is unidentified). It tells how people wanted to have a finer and larger bell than any other parish, so they ordered an enormous one from a foundry abroad, to be called 'Great Tom of Kentsham'. In due course, a ship arrived in England, bringing bells for cathedrals at Lincoln, York, and Christchurch (all called Tom), and one for Kentsham, 'which was the greatest Tom of all'. The first three were safely disembarked, and then came the turn of the Kentsham bell:

Little by little they raised him, and prepared to draw him to the shore; but just in the midst of the work the captain grew so anxious and excited that he swore an oath; that very minute the ropes that held the bell snapped in two, and the great Tom of Kentsham slipped over the ship's side into the water, and rolled away to the bottom of the sea.

Then the people went to the cunning man and asked what they should do, and he said: 'Take six yoke of white milch-kine which have never borne the yoke, and take fresh withy bands which have never been used before, and let no man speak a word either good or bad until the bell is at the top of the hill.'

This they did, and all went well till the bell was nearly at the top:

Now the captain had been wild with grief when he saw that he had caused his precious freight to be lost in the waters just as they reached the shore, and when he beheld it recovered again and so nearly placed in safety, he could not restrain his joy, but sang out merrily,

> 'In spite of all the devils in hell,
> We have got to land old Kentsham bell.'

Instantly the withy bands broke in the midst, and the bell bounded back again down the sloping hillside, rolling over and over, faster and faster, with unearthly clanging, till it sank far away in the very depths of the sea, and no man has seen it since; but many have heard it tolling underneath the waters, and if you go there you may hear it too.

A bell may also actively protest if mistreated or offended. At Bosham, Sussex, a stolen bell sinks the boat in which it is being carried off; one from Barlinch Priory, Somerset, refused to ring when forcibly transferred to Exeter Cathedral. Above all, a church bell shows a moral sense: the bell-seekers fail not simply because they break silence, but because they prematurely boast of success, and, most of all, because they mention 'all the devils in hell'. The same couplet, with appropriate variation of the place-name, occurs in many of the legends.

Religious and magical elements mingle in these tales. The person who explains the conditions for recovering the bell is not a priest, but a 'cunning man' or a witch; however, the animals used must be pure white, symbolizing holiness. At Marden, Herefordshire, the cattle are harnessed with yew wood and rowan; both are traditionally said to repel evil, but whereas yew is a Christian symbol of everlasting life, rowan is used in folk magic only.

Other recurrent tales concern bells of Sunken Churches, and travellers guided home by the sound of a curfew bell.

The Bloody Hand

A number of legends have arisen as popular explanations of heraldry, among them stories attached to the Eagle and Child of the Stanleys, to Walworth's dagger in the City of London's arms, and to the *three boys' heads couped at the shoulder, each having a snake wreathed round his neck, proper* of the Herefordshire Vaughans, supposedly derived from an ancestor born with a snake round his neck. However, none are as sensational as tales of the 'bloody hand', which form part of a corpus of legends concerning the punishment of 'wicked gentry'.

A notable example concerns the Lytteltons or Lyttletons of Hagley in Worcestershire, specifically Thomas Lyttelton (1744–79), 'the wicked Lord Lyttelton', also the subject of a well-known ghost story attached to Epsom, Surrey.

A contributor wrote to *Notes and Queries* in March 1856:

Being at Hagley, some time since, and conversing with a villager about the Lyttelton family, I was gravely informed that on account of the misdeeds of Thomas Lord Lyttelton . . . the Lord Lytteltons were compelled to have a 'bloody hand' in their arms; and that their arms being painted on a board, with the bloody hand very conspicuous thereon, were placed over the door of the hall; and I was moreover informed, that his lordship dared not remove it for twelve months. This board, I found, was placed there just after the death of the late lord, and was nothing more or less than a hatchment. I was also told that the hand was to be smaller every generation, until it entirely disappeared.

He had heard a similar tradition concerning the Holtes (or Holts) of Aston Hall, Warwickshire:

In one of the windows of Aston Church . . . are the arms of the Holts, baronets of Aston; and there . . . the hand has been painted minus one finger; and to explain this, I was told that one of the Holts, having committed some evil deed, was compelled to place the bloody hand in his arms, and transmit the same to his descendants, who were allowed to take one finger off for each generation, until all the fingers and thumbs being deducted, it might at length be dispensed with altogether!

Other contributors responded with stories of 'Bloody Baker', at Cranbrook, Kent, and of the Vincents at Stoke D'Abernon, Surrey. In this last case, the contributor had been told the following concerning a 'bloody hand' on a monument in the church:

Two young brothers of the family of Vincent, the elder of whom had just come into possession of the estate, were out shooting on Fairmile Common, about two miles from the village; they had put up several birds, but had not been able to get a single shot, when the elder swore with an oath that he would fire at whatever they next met with. They had not

gone much further before the miller of a mill near at hand
(and which is still standing) passed them, and made some
trifling remark. As soon as he had got by, the younger brother
jokingly reminded the elder of his oath, whereupon the latter
immediately fired at the miller, who fell dead upon the spot.
Young Vincent escaped to his home, and by the influence of
his family, backed by large sums of money, no effective steps
were taken to apprehend him, and he was concealed in the
'Nunnery' on his estate for some years, when death put a
period to the insupportable anguish of his mind. To commem-
orate his rash act and his untimely death, this 'bloody hand'
was placed on his monument.

At Wateringbury church, in Kent, a 'bloody hand'
story accounted for the arms on a funeral hatchment,
and at Church-Gresley, Derbyshire, another was told
of a table in the hall. In a Suffolk story attached to
Homersfield Bridge, on which only three of four original
'bloody hands' could be seen, they were connected with
a spirit 'laid' under the bridge for as long as the water
flowed under the arch. They represented the Adairs,
who, like the Lytteltons and Holts, were allowed to
reduce the mark of shame in each generation, in the
Adairs' case by taking off one hand.

Norfolk tradition said that the Berneys had been forced
to wear a 'bloody hand', because one of them 'whipped
a boy to dead'; later the tradition was attached specifically
to Sir Berney Brograve of Waxham Hall.

The truth is that Sir Berney's grandfather was created
baronet in the reign of James I, Sir Berney himself in
1791, and here, as in other instances of the legend, the

'bloody hand' is the badge of baronetcy. The title of *Baronet* Hereditary was introduced by James I in 1611 to raise money for the plantation of Ulster, and baronets of England and Ireland (1611–1707), of Great Britain (1707–1801), and latterly of the United Kingdom are entitled to augment their arms with *a sinister hand appaumé coupé at the wrist and erect, gules*, the badge of the Ulster King-at-Arms. Known as the Red Hand of Ulster, it was formerly the badge of the O'Neils. This itself was accounted for by a legend. The leader of an expedition to Ireland had declared that whoever first landed on its shore should possess that territory which he touched. O'Neil, from whom descended the princes of Ulster, seeing another boat likely to land, cut off his hand and threw it onto the coast.

Boadicea's Graves

The revolt against Rome in AD 60–61 led by the queen of the Iceni was a disaster, effectively the end of her tribe as a power. Perhaps only in Britain, with its long tradition of celebrating military fiascos – Catraeth (sixth century), Maldon (991), the Charge of the Light Brigade (1880) – would she be cast as a heroine.

The Roman historian Tacitus called her Boudicca: Tudor and Stuart historians favoured Bonduca and Voadicia. In the eighteenth and nineteenth centuries, she was generally called Boadicea, and this is what passed into local tradition. Correctly, say philologists, her name is Boudica or Boudiga, meaning 'victory'.

The events leading to Boudica's final battle and her death are narrated elsewhere. As Tacitus does not say where the last battle took place, earlier generations speculated more or less widely: it was said in Middlesex to have been fought on Stanmore Common, but in Essex at Ambresbury Banks, while Londoners said it gave its name to Battle Bridge Road, behind King's Cross Station.

Dio Cassius's ending to the story is an anti-climax: he says simply that, after the battle, Boudica fell ill and died. Tacitus, however, says she fled the field and ended her life by poison. This scenario has been generally accepted, as suicide is most dramatically satisfying (compare

Cleopatra). Certainly suicide would have been the *Roman* way.

Suicide it was, then, and in Essex it was said that she killed herself near Ambresbury Banks and her ghost wanders there – but she also drives her spectral chariot in Lincolnshire near Cammeringham. As to her place of burial, one seventeenth-century antiquary opined that Stonehenge was her funeral monument; later tradition said it was Gop Carn, Gwaenysgor, the largest cairn in Wales. Middlesex people claimed that, after her defeat on Stanmore Common, she was buried in a tumulus traditionally known as 'Boadicea's Grave'. In Victorian London, opinion was divided as to whether she lay buried under King's Cross Station, or in another 'Boadicea's Grave' in Parliament Hill Fields. In Norfolk, she supposedly lies under barrows in two different places, at Quidenham and Garboldisham Heath.

Alternative explanations attached to some of these sites suggest that older traditions were overlaid by the later assignment of the graves to Boadicea. For she has not always been a heroine. The Welsh monk Gildas, writing in the sixth century, called her a 'treacherous lioness'. She was lost to sight during the Middle Ages, but hailed in the reign of Elizabeth I as a forerunner of the Virgin Queen. Dio's description of her offered seductive parallels: like Elizabeth, Boudica was red-haired and gorgeously dressed, wearing a many-coloured tunic and a gold torque round her neck; and she harangued her troops, like Elizabeth at Tilbury. The Tudors underlined the message, dressing Boudica to look like Elizabeth in pictures. Under the Commonwealth, however, she was again out of favour, John Milton in his *History of Britain* (1670) condemning her as a 'distracted woman, with as mad a crew at her heels'.

The later view of her as a warrior and patriot only got under way with William Cowper's 'Ode on Boadicea' in the late eighteenth century. She became immensely popular in the reign of Queen Victoria, the atrocities recorded of her by Roman historians – and shown by archaeology to have been not entirely propaganda – being glossed over. Tacitus had presented her motives for the revolt as personal:

. . . she did not now come forward as one of noble descent, fighting for her kingdom and her wealth: rather she presented herself as an ordinary woman, striving to avenge her lost liberty, her lash-tortured body, and the violated honour of her daughters.

The Victorians chose to see her both as an outraged matron and defender of her people. As a queen who was also called 'Victoria', she was a useful symbol for the empire builders, a phase culminating in 1902 when the chariot-borne statue of her by Thomas Thorneycroft was erected on the Embankment.

Each age has remade the British queen according to its own preoccupations: for Lewis Spence, writing on the threshold of the Second World War, she was one of the valiant 'who have died for the right to champion their native soil against foreign aggression'; in the later twentieth century, she became a feminist symbol of independent womanhood, or was represented as a

'Celtic' ruling queen like Cartimandua of the Brigantes (despite the fact that the Brigantes's matriarchal society was a pre-Celtic survival). We still know very little about the real Boudica, though Dio remarks, 'She was . . . possessed of greater intelligence than usually belongs to women.'

Whatever she was like, there is no doubt that the traditions of 'Boadicea's Graves' date from the romantic eighteenth and nineteenth centuries, and do not represent 'folk memories' of her historical burial place. Knowing this does not diminish their glamour: she has become a national icon, and human nature needs visible shrines to its heroes.

Bogey Beasts

The distinction between bogey beasts and hobgoblins is blurred. One characteristic of Shakespeare's Puck or Robin Goodfellow, whom most think of as humanoid, is his horse-laugh 'Ho! Ho! Ho!' when pulling off mischief. But hobgoblins like Robin were thought to be shape-shifters. Ben Jonson's Robin Goodfellow declares:

> Sometimes I meete them like a man,
>> Sometimes an ox, sometimes a hound,
> And to a horse I turn me can,
>> To trip and trot them round.

Conversely, bogey beasts could also 'meete them like a man'. W. Hylton Dyer Longstaffe, in his *History . . . of Darlington* (1854), says that at Thirsk, Yorkshire, was a stream known as 'White-lass-beck', the 'White-lass' being the ghost of a murdered girl. However, she was a shape-shifter, 'turning into a white dog, and an ugly animal which comes rattling into the town with a tremendous clitter-my-clatter, and is there styled a barguest'. The Hedley Kow of Hedley on the Hill, Northumberland, deluded two young men into following their sweethearts, until they found themselves in a quagmire and the girls vanished 'with the most unfeminine Ha! Ha!' The Hedley Kow could also 'turn him to a horse', a transformation with a long history: about 1211, Gervase of Tilbury described creatures called 'grants' as 'like foals of a year old'. This is the shag-foal or Tatterfoal of whom the Northamptonshire poet John Clare (1821) writes:

Old Ball – You mean – the shagg'd foal. Its a common tradition in village that the devil often appears in the form of a shagg'd foal: and a man in our parish firmly believes that he saw him in that character.

A shag-foal is a foal whose baby fuzz is giving way to its adult horsehair, hence the tatters.

In Northamptonshire there was a proverb, 'To laugh like old Bogie'. Sir Walter Scott, in *Border Minstrelsy* (first published 1802), mentions the 'goblin' of northern England, 'which, in . . . Durham and Newcastle . . . had the name of *Barguest*; but, in the country villages . . . *Brag*. He usually ended his mischievous frolics with a horse-laugh.' The Pelton Brag, Co. Durham, often appeared as a coach horse. After dumping a man riding it into a pond, it ran off 'setting up a great nicker and laugh'.

Other bogey beasts chose different guises. The Portobello Brag in Co. Durham appeared as an ass; the 'Hazelrigg Dunnie' frequenting Cuddie's Cave, Northumberland, appeared as a dun-coloured pony or horse, but also as a donkey; and about 1840, a shepherd in Kirton-in-Lindsey, Lincolnshire, had a 'Shagged-Foal' 'sum'ate like a donkey' place its nose on his shoulder. At Brigg, also Lincolnshire, the Lackey Causey Calf is self-explanatory; and the Pelton Brag looked like a calf with a bushy tail and white handkerchief round its neck. In William Hone's *Every-Day Book* (1826), a man walking from Grassington towards Linton, Yorkshire, tells of hearing something pass 'brush, brush, brush, wi' chains rattlin'' and knowing it was a barguest. Following it, he saw 'a grit thing like a sheep, but . . . larger . . . and . . . woolly like'. This sounds like the bogey beast SHUCK. The 'Shock' at Melton, Suffolk, had a donkey's head and smooth hide, but hung on the toll gate like the Cambridgeshire Shug Monkey. At Glassensikes, Co. Durham, the bogey shifted between human form and white cats, rabbits, and white or black dogs.

Bogey beasts can also take inanimate forms: the shepherd who saw the Shagged-Foal near Kirton-in-Lindsey saw it reappear as 'a luminous mass'; the Glassensikes bogey once manifested as 'a great *gulph of fire*'. The Hedley Kow could be a truss of straw; the bogey at Glowrowram, Co. Durham, could appear as a sheet or a woolpack; Longstaffe relates of Norton, Yorkshire: 'Two gentlemen (one a very dear friend of mine . . . now deceased) saw near a water an exquisitely beautiful white heifer turn into *a roll of Irish linen*.'

Shape-shifting is one of the things that distinguishes bogey beasts from true Black Dogs, but often it is some unusual feature, such as colour, as when a Lincolnshire man said that in 1894, as a boy, he went to steal corn for his horses but was prevented by seeing 'a yellow smooth-haired dog the size of a calf'. Consequently it is hard to say if the black dog of Dog Lane, Gillingham, Norfolk, was thought to be a Black Dog or Shuck, who also had regular 'beats', as did the shag-foal in

Lincolnshire, where a bridle road between Benniworth and Donington-on-Bain was known as 'Shag-foal lane'; and the bullbeggars who gave their name to Bullbeggers Lane, Hertfordshire.

Mabel Peacock reported the comment 'You don't hear of inquests being held on people who have been killed by . . . boggarts.' But the Melton Shock savaged someone's thumb; Shuck would sometimes attack horses; and northern brags, like the dangerous kelpies, which often took horse form, sometimes enticed or carried people into quagmires, rivers, and ponds. It was his spitefulness towards strangers that led to the Capelthwaite at Beetham, Westmorland, being laid. Bogey beasts, unlike nursery bogeys invented to frighten children, were for adults 'real' night terrors.

The Book-Fish

One of the greatest 'marvels' ever to set Cambridge by the ears was the incident of the 'Book-Fish'.

The story is told in *Vox Piscis: or, the Book-Fish* . . . (1627):

On Midsummer Eue last past 1626, a Codfish being brought to the Fish-market of Cambridge and there cut vp . . ., in the depth of the mawe of the fish was found wrapped in a peice [*sic*] of Canuase [canvas], a booke . . . much soyled, and defaced, and couered ouer with a kind of slime & congealed matter. This Booke was then and there beheld by many with admiration, and by *Beniamin Prim* the Batchelors Beadle (who also was present at the opening of the fish) was presently carried to the Vice-chancellor of the Vniuersity, who . . . examined the truth of the particulars before mentioned.

The book's leaves were brittle from being 'parboyled' by the heat of the cod-fish's maw: 'And therefore it seemeth most probable, that vpon some wrack this booke lying (perhaps manie years) in the pocket of some man, that was cast away, was swallowed by the Cod, and that it lay for a good space of time in the fishes belly.'

On being cleaned up, the book was found to contain three religious pieces written in prison by the Protestant Reformer John Frith (*c.*1503–33). 'The Preparation to the

Cross and to Death', 'A Mirrour, or, Glasse to know thy selfe' and 'A Briefe Instruction, to teach a person willingly to die, and not to feare death' (the latter sometimes attributed to Richard Tracy). In 1533, Frith was burnt at the stake for denying that the doctrines of Purgatory and Transubstantiation were necessary articles of faith. He was important in the history of the English Reformation as having been the first to maintain the Protestant view of the sacrament of Communion, that 'Christ's natural blood and body are in Heaven, not here'.

The writer of the introduction to *Vox Piscis* says that the finding of the book-fish 'is to bee accounted rather maruellous than miraculous' – in other words, this was *not* the supernatural intervening in human affairs in order (belatedly) to make manifest divine approval of the Reformist views of Frith. But no doubt many saw special significance in the contents and that was why the university authorities swiftly brought out a reprint, *Vox Piscis* itself, enlivening the text with a woodcut showing the fish-woman's stall, the fish, the book, and the knife.

That is always supposing that the story is true. Although *Vox Piscis* represents the events it describes as of recent occurrence, several suspicious circumstances surround the finding of the book, not least the coinciden-tal presence of authority in the shape not only of Ben-jamin Prim but also of various scholars of the university who immediately wrote to their friends about it, 'relating the particulars of this accident whereof themselues were eye-witnesses'. And how many of these 'eye-witnesses' saw the same events as Mr Mead, the Fellow of Christ-church College, who afterwards wrote, 'I saw all with mine own eyes . . .; only I saw not the opening of the fish, which not many did, being upon the fish-woman's stall in the market . . .'? It is all very well for Mr Mead to say 'He that had his nose as near as I yester morning, would have been persuaded there was no imposture . . .', but of course there was opportunity for it.

'Strange to say,' comments Robert Chambers in his *Book of Days* (1863–4), before being confined in the Tower of London, Frith had been held in an Oxford fish cellar, where fellow prisoners had died from fumes given off by decaying salted fish – a coincidence to strain credulity. Perhaps *Vox Piscis* was a donnish joke. But whoever wrote it knew that stories of strange things found in fish were perennially popular.

Some of the earliest stories concern rings lost and found again in fish. The subject is still regarded as newsworthy. Jack Rose, in *Tales and Tall Stories* (1992), reports that a small pocketbook found in a pint bottle cut from the stomach of a ling landed from the Lowestoft trawler *Sybil* at Aberdeen contained a farewell to his wife, written on 24 January 1886 by William Jenson of the schooner *Anna* of Bangor. In the *Lowestoft Weekly Press* on 1 October 1887 appeared a letter reporting that 'on Monday last' (20 September) a Lowestoft fishing vessel landed a cod of an unusual size, which was prepared for cooking. 'Upon opening the fish . . . to the utter astonishment of the Master and part of the crew, a new born infant, in a perfect state, presented itself to their almost unbelieving eyes.'

Twentieth-century newspapers publish more realistic claims: *The Times* of 24 June 1995 printed the story of a fisherman who caught a bass in Southampton Water and found a lady's ring from about 1850 inside it; and a still-ticking watch found inside a cod was reported in the *Eastern Daily Press* on 2 March 1993. However, whether any or all of the above are truthful accounts or tall tales is another matter, particularly when they are viewed in the light of a story told by Fletcher Bassett, in *Legends and Superstitions of the Sea and Sailors* (1885), who writes, 'A shark cut open at Marseilles is said to have contained a man, clad in armor, in its stomach, and another, a horse.'

The Brown Lady

The Brown Lady of Raynham has reputedly haunted Raynham Hall, at East Rainham, for nearly three centuries. In *The Night-Side of Nature* (1848), Mrs Crowe reports:

The Hon. H. W. – told me that a friend of his . . . had often seen her, and had one day inquired of his host, 'Who was the lady in brown that he had met frequently on the stairs?' . . . Many persons have seen her.

Charles Loftus, the brother-in-law and cousin of Lord Charles Townshend, owner of Raynham, in his autobiography *My Youth by Sea and Land* (1876), gives his account of the ghost, 'who, in 1842 and 1844, caused such excitement among the inmates, visitors and servants'. After saying that he did not himself see her, he relates the experience of three young men of the family, cousins, staying in the house in October and November 1855. Encountering her one night on the stairs, they pursued her, but when they had her cornered she waved her hand and disappeared. Next morning, after hearing their adventure, one of the family exclaimed:

'This is exactly what occurred to me – the same appearance on the stairs, with precisely the same dress, and high-heeled shoes. I made notes of it all at the time. And, oh! the awful expression of those glazed, hollow eyes, and the parchment-colour of her pinched cheeks! Who can she be? I said nothing about this when it occurred to me in 1844, but it is perfectly true.'

Loftus, who was a Townshend on his mother's side, knew the apparition as the 'family ghost' (his words), Lady Dorothy Walpole, sister of Sir Robert Walpole. Loftus calls her 'Lady Dorothy', and refers to her 'well-known face and figure', recognizable from a portrait at Raynham showing her in the dress in which she often appeared, 'of a brown silk brocade spangled with gold'.

Lady Dorothy married the second Viscount Towns-hend in 1713, but the marriage seems to have been unhappy. Norfolk tradition said she was a young and beautiful lady, forced to marry an old man against her will, but the antiquary Walter Rye remarks that never was there a tradition with less foundation. Dorothy's husband sent their children to be brought up by his mother at Raynham, and some suggest that it was to find them that, after her death from smallpox in 1726, she returned to the Hall. However, Charles Loftus writes:

Two reasons were given by her family why she could not rest; one was that she was offended because her family had not been ennobled, and the other that some of her husband's family possessed wealth to which she conceived herself entitled. So that on one side she hated the Walpole, and on the other the Loftus, family on their appearance at Raynham.

According to his daughter Florence, Captain Marryat (1792–1848), who lived at Langham, spoke of seeing the Brown Lady. Holding up the lighted lamp she carried, she 'grinned in a malicious and diabolical manner', so enraging him that he fired his revolver at her. She immediately vanished and the bullet lodged in a door.

Though Loftus speaks of the haunting having ceased, Florence notes, 'I have heard that she haunts the premises to this day', and indeed she reputedly appeared on 19 September 1936, when a photographer, Indra Shira, and his assistant Captain Provand, were photographing the oak staircase. Shira suddenly called out to Provand to press the trigger, and Provand had no time to see what Shira saw: a ghostly figure coming down the stairs towards them. However, a misty shape resembling a woman in a long dress appeared on their photograph published on 16 December 1936, in *Country Life*.

Lady Dorothy also haunted Houghton Hall, built on the site of her old family home. According to Walter Rye, George IV, as Prince Regent, saw a little lady dressed in brown, with dishevelled hair and ashen face, by his bed in the State Bedroom and 'with many oaths' declared, 'I will not pass another hour in this accursed house, for I have seen that what I hope to God I may never see again.'

William Dutt, in *Highways and Byways in East Anglia* (1901), says the 'Browne Lady' was introduced from Houghton into Raynham 'when one of Sir Robert Walpole's sisters married a Marquis of Townshend'. This suggests that some people believed her to be a spectre who moved to Raynham with Dorothy on her marriage, like a handful of other family apparitions that were passed down in the female line.

The change of haunt is characteristic of spirits attached to families such as banshees and dynastic White Ladies, both of which normally serve as death omens. This may be why not everyone calls her a *Brown* Lady: Walter Rye refers to her as the *Grey* Lady, and in *The Perlustrations of Yarmouth* (1875) she is called the *White* Lady, and said to have appeared a few days before the death of the Marquis of Townshend in 1863. Possibly one sort of apparition has evolved into another, a hereditary death-warning into a historical ghost.

Cunning Men

'Cunning men' were not legendary figures like Master Magicians, but real-life experts in occult matters with an important role in everyday life, whose activities are well attested in written accounts from the sixteenth century to the early twentieth, together with newspaper reports and advertisements. Their female counterparts were usually called 'wise women', or sometimes 'witches' – in the latter case, it would be clear from the context that their powers were benevolent, not destructive.

The power most frequently mentioned is magical healing for humans or animals, through verbal charms, material charms, ritual actions, medicinal herbs, or any combination of these. If the sufferer suspected witchcraft, the cunning man could identify the witch by divination, and provide counter-spells. One was to take an animal's heart, stick it with pins or thorns, and roast it; this was chiefly used to counter disease in farm animals, and there are detailed accounts from nineteenth-century Yorkshire and Durham. Another, for humans, was to fill a bottle with the sick person's urine, adding pins or knotted threads, and either bury or slowly boil it. Cunning Murrell of Hadleigh, Essex, and Jenkins of Weobley, Herefordshire, were famous for defeating witches.

Many cunning men also located lost or stolen property, and might identify the thief, or lead their client to do so, by looking into water or a mirror, or consulting the stars. They also used love divinations, and supplied love charms. Occasionally, they were asked to help find buried treasure.

Folklorists in North Yorkshire and Durham in the latter half of the nineteenth century were told many anecdotes about a 'wizard' called Wrightson who had lived at Stokesley in Yorkshire around the beginning of that century, and was consulted by people from miles around. He said he owed his powers to being the seventh son of a seventh daughter, but that they only worked if he was fasting. His moral character was said to have been very bad, yet the people of Stokesley were so much in awe of him that they often invited him to be godfather to their children, on which occasions he used to appear in church in flamboyant, if old-fashioned, attire: a scarlet coat, a long white waistcoat, a shirt with a starched frill, crimson knee-breeches, and white stockings.

The tales about him mostly concerned his second sight. If someone came to ask his help for, say, a sick cow, before the man had uttered a word Wrightson would tell him what she looked like and what her symptoms were. He knew what people coming to see him had said on the way, especially if it was a critical or sceptical comment about himself. For example, a miner whose shirt had disappeared while he was down the pit set off at once, with a friend called Elijah, to ask Wrightson if he could tell who had stolen it. On the way, it being a warm day, Elijah took off his own overcoat and left it by the road at a place called West House, saying that if the wizard could tell where the coat was, they would believe whatever he said about the missing shirt. But as soon as they walked in at the door, Wrightson said, 'What hast'ee done wi' thy coat, Elijah? I think thee'st left it at West House. Thinkst'ee t'wise man knaws aught about t'shart?' They were struck dumb with astonishment. He then described the shirt, and said the owner would find it at his home – and so it was, for someone had taken it by mistake, and had already brought it back.

He could probably hypnotize. It is said that two men on their way to Stokesley Fair decided to have 'a bit of sport with Old Wrightson'. When they reached his house he asked them in, and offered them chairs in front of the fire, piling fuel on till it blazed fiercely. The visitors tried to push their chairs back a bit, but found that nothing they could do would shift them; they found themselves fixed immoveably to their chairs, and their chairs equally fixed to the floor, and all the while the fire was getting hotter and hotter. So there they sat, roasting and sweating, until the wizard at length set them free. 'Away wi' ye to the fair,' said he, 'and tell a' your friends the sport ye've had wi' auld Wrightson.'

This exploit could be rationally explained as hypnotism; so could the power of a supposed wizard nicknamed 'Pigtail Bridger' at Crowborough, Sussex. He was so named because of the old-fashioned way he wore his hair: his clothes, too, were eccentric, invariably including a long scarf wound several times round his neck, knickerbockers, and bare feet in carpet slippers. As he was tall, heavy-built, and fierce-looking, he inspired a good deal of fear. It was said he had some way to keep a man stuck motionless for as long as he chose, though fully conscious; this he would do to annoy and ridicule anyone who angered him, and to punish workmen on his farm – for instance, by eating up their food himself while they watched helplessly.

Other cunning men were credited with the opposite power – an ability to make people run about or dance against their will. A tale illustrating this is told of the man at Weobley, Herefordshire, whom Mrs Leather calls 'Jenkins', though saying it was not his real name: annoyed because the landlady of an inn had overcharged him for food and drink, he caused her and her servants to run round and round the table for hours, unable to touch the coins he had laid there.

The Danes

Thomas Sternberg, writing in 1851, says that in Northamptonshire in his time people spoke of old coins they found as 'Dane's-Money':

To the same source they ascribe the origin of the most of the ancient remains; and innumerable legends are still current of battles, burnings, &c., in which the Danes play the most conspicuous part. There would appear still to remain a traditional remembrance of their oppression.

The argument for a 'traditional remembrance' of the Danes in Northamptonshire would be strong, given the historical Danish occupation, were it not for the fact that counties never part of the Danelaw make similar claims. Early antiquaries, ignorant of prehistory, solved most dating problems connected with ancient sites by reference to Romans or Danes, and so, it seems, did locals. The 'Danes' – by which was meant any Scandinavian invader – were 'remembered' throughout England as the archetypal enemy.

Natural features like Danes' Hole at Nab Hill, Sedgefield, were thought to be Danish skulking places, and hillforts were attributed to them right across the country, from Warham Camp, Norfolk, to Danesborough in the Quantock Hills, Somerset, and Cornish hill-forts and cliff-castles like Caer Dane near Perranzabuloe, Castle-an-Dinas, Ludgvan, and Treryn Dinas at Treen. The Danes were also credited with erecting megalithic monuments, including the Rollright Stones, Oxfordshire.

Battle sites were deduced from place-names: there was allegedly a great battle against the Danes at Drayton, near Norwich, the ashes of the slain being buried in a meadow called 'Bloodsdale'; another was supposedly fought at a barrow on Bloodmere Hill, Pakefield, Suffolk.

The diarist Samuel Pepys records that, when he visited Rochester in Kent in 1661, he was told that the west doors of the cathedral were covered with 'Dane-skins', traditionally said to be the skins of Danes flayed alive for sacrilege, the same story being told of Worcester Cathedral, Westminster Abbey, and several parish churches, including that of Hadstock, Essex.

Living people, too, were drawn into this pseudo-history: the Danes were said to have settled in several places in the West Country, their descendants known by their red hair. Robert Hunt in 1881 reported that, in Sennen Cove, Cornwall, there was a colony of red-haired people – some still alive in his day – with whom other local inhabitants refused to marry. In the outlying villages, red-haired people were looked down on, and 'red-haired Dane' was a term of abuse. In the Quantocks, also supposedly settled by Danes, a redhead might be insulted as a 'Dane's bastard'.

In Northamptonshire, antiquaries had a field day with imaginary Danes. Of the hill-fort at Rainsborough, Morton writes, 'some Gentlemen in the Neighbourhood would have it *Dainesborough* . . . but we are not to take notice of that', yet nonetheless thinks it was made by the Danes in pursuance of 'their old accustomed way of Burning and Plunder' and is himself seduced by false etymology when it comes to Heathencote, 'which . . . I doubt not had . . . its Name from the *Danes* (usually call'd *Heathen* Men in the *Saxon* Annals)'.

Antiquarian learning leaked into folk history at many points: of the hill-fort of Hunsbury Hill, Morton says, 'Enquiring of some of the antientest Inhabitants of *North-ampton*, by whom they thought the Entrenchment at *Hunsborough* was made, they answered by the *Danes*.' Again: 'That *Stean, Tutsbury*, and other Towns . . . were destroyed by the *Danes*, is firmly believ'd by all the Neighbourhood.' There was a supposed battle on Wittering Heath, 'wherein . . . the *Danes* receiv'd a memorable Overthrow', and at Borough Hill 'a Tradition of a Battel fought between the *Danes* and *Saxons*'. Commenting on the number of human bones found 'in Ditching . . . as also nigh the round Hill at *Lilbourn*', Morton records a 'Tradition of the Countrey people' of a like battle there: 'But . . .'tis the way of the Vulgar with us to attribute all such Actions to the *Danes*.'

It is debatable if 'remembrance' is involved in *any* tradition concerning Danes. One at least is mythological. That flowers may be born of blood is an idea found almost worldwide, and in England sites of battles with the Danes were supposedly revealed by the flourishing there of 'Danesblood', 'Danewort', or 'Daneweed'. In the seventeenth century, John Aubrey writes of Gatton, Surrey:

This place is renowned for a great slaughter committed on the plundering Danes by the women; and as a confirmation of this tradition the vulgar show the herb called Dane-wort in great plenty, which they fancy to have sprung from the Danish blood.

At Borough Hill, what Defoe identified as 'Dane-weed' was *Eryngium campestre*. Elsewhere, plants supposed to have sprung from the blood of Danes include the snake's head fritillary (*Fritillaria meleagris*), the pasque flower (*Anemone pulsatilla*), and the clustered bell-flower (*Campanula glomerata*), but most commonly, as on the Bartlow Hills, Essex, the dwarf elder.

The dwarf elder (*Sambucus ebulus*) is still locally known as Danewort in Berkshire, as Dane Weed in Suffolk and Somerset. Curiously enough, country people held the same view of it in Sweden. Before setting out on his Gotland Expedition in 1741, Linnaeus was asked to look at the plant called *Manna Blod* ('Man's Blood') and was disappointed to find that it was only dwarf elder, reputedly sprung from the blood of Swedes and Danes fallen in battle.

Dick Turpin

The historical facts behind the Turpin legend are well documented, and it is equally clear when, and by whom, the popular image was created.

Dick Turpin was a butcher's son, born in Hempstead, Essex, in 1705. He joined a group of violent criminals active on the outskirts of London in 1734/5. Well armed, they would break into a house, and threaten, beat up, or burn the occupants until they handed over their money. In 1735, most of the group were captured, and hanged or transported. Turpin remained at large, but turned to a different crime, namely highway robbery. On 1 May 1737, in Whitechapel, he accidently shot one of his own comrades while firing at a man whose horse he had stolen; he then hid in Epping Forest, where he killed a man who tried to arrest him.

Using the alias 'John Palmer', Turpin moved to Lincolnshire, then to Essex, and finally to Yorkshire. In October 1738, 'Palmer' was arrested for threatening to shoot a man during a quarrel, and trading in stolen horses. Horse theft was a capital crime, so he was imprisoned in York Castle to await trial. His real identity was still unknown, but by sheer chance he was identified by someone who recognized his handwriting. On 22 March 1739, Turpin was found guilty of horse-stealing and condemned to death; if he had been acquitted, he would have been transferred to London to meet further charges.

Once Turpin's identity was known, his notoriety drew crowds to York Castle, where, as the contemporary account records, 'he continu'd his mirthful humour to the last, spending his time in joking, drinking, and telling stories'. On the day of his execution he put up a equally good show. Well dressed, and 'bowing to spectators as he passed', he was driven in a cart to the gallows. He mounted the ladder boldly, declaring that he was indeed guilty of the horse thefts, and also of the murder in Epping Forest and various robberies. Finally he 'threw himself off the ladder and expired directly', showing 'as much intrepidity and unconcern as if he had been taking horse to go on a journey'.

It was a gallant end to a nasty career, suitable for a legendary hero. Yet Turpin only achieved this status almost a hundred years later, thanks to Harrison Ainsworth's novel *Rookwood* (1834). Ainsworth presented highwaymen in general, and Turpin in particular, as romantic, fearless, and gentlemanly. He also virtually invented the most famous episode in the Turpin legend: the hero's non-stop ride from London to York on Black Bess, and her pathetic death at the very gates of the city. His only sources were a bare mention in a ballad published in 1825 of Turpin riding 'his black mare Bess' on Hounslow Heath, and the older tradition of a highwayman riding at breakneck speed from Gad's Hill, Kent, to York, to establish an alibi.

Ainsworth's fiction was soon mistaken for fact, spawning a host of local legends. By 1911, his biographer S. M. Ellis could write:

All along the great North Road the legend is truth; every village through which the highwayman galloped (in the imagination of Ainsworth) during that famous ride has its own peculiar tale and relic of Turpin's feat. From Tottenham to Ware – from Huntingdon to Stamford – from Newark to York – a volume of Turpinian anecdotes can be collected from innkeepers and ostlers; here, you may learn how Turpin refreshed his mare with strong ale and see the very tankard he used; and there, how he leaped the five-bar toll-gate!

The Spaniards in Hampstead goes further, claiming that he was born there, watched passing coaches from an upstairs room, stabled Black Bess in a nearby toll house, and had an escape tunnel to another inn. The latest scholar to examine the Turpin story, James Sharpe, comments:

[T]here are, indeed, so many pubs alleging Turpin associations that if all their claims were true, the career of England's most famous highwayman would have been passed in a combination of perpetual motion and a permanent alcoholic haze.

The Doones

Murray's Handbook for . . . Devon (1879) advises anyone visiting Exmoor to prepare by studying R. D. Blackmore's romance *Lorna Doone* (1869), and gives the following account of the famous Doone clan:

. . . in a bottom called the Warren are some remains of a building which was once the stronghold of the *Doones of Badgeworthy*, a daring band of robbers who infested the borders of the moor in the time of the Commonwealth . . . They are said . . . to have entered Devonshire about the time of Cromwell's usurpation. It is certain that for many years they were a terror to the neighbourhood of Lynton . . . At length, however, they committed so savage a murder that the whole country was aroused, and a large part of the peasantry . . . captured the entire gang. This ended the career of the Doones, for they were . . . tried for their numerous crimes, and deservedly executed.

Stories of the Doones were current on Exmoor at least fifty years before *Lorna Doone* appeared. Blackmore says in his preface that the 'nurse-tales' of his childhood went into its making, among them 'the savage deeds of the outlaw Doones in the depth of Bagworthy Forest . . . the plain John Ridd's Herculean power, and . . . the exploits of Tom Faggus'. Although its background is the Monmouth Rebellion and other seventeenth-century concerns, at the heart of the novel is John's love for Lorna and his growth to manhood, each stage marked by some confrontation with the 'bloody Doones'. Though Lorna herself was probably invented by Blackmore, minor characters such as Judge Jeffreys are historical, and so may be some of the leading players, even if their exploits are not.

No doubt Blackmore's main sources were indeed tales heard in childhood. Between 1837 and 1843 he attended Blundell's school in Tiverton (the same school as John Ridd), where he may have also heard stories from Exmoor classmates. Besides oral traditions, tales about the Doones and the highwayman Tom Faggus evidently circulated in manuscript from at least 1842 and were written out by girls of the National School, Lynton, in the 1850s. A story entitled 'The Doones of Exmoor' appeared in the *Leisure Hour* for September–October 1863, and may have jogged Blackmore's memory.

So who were the Doones? In 1901, Ida M. Browne (under the pseudonym Audrie Doone) contributed the article 'The Original Doones of Exmoor' to the *West Somerset Free Press*, which brought it out as a pamphlet. She says the family name was originally spelled Doune, later Doone, and finally Doon; and that, on being exiled from Scotland in 1620, they settled in the Oare valley. Here they were 'more or less' hated and feared by the countryside until their return to Perthshire in 1699. 'Such is the story attached to our family.'

Not everyone has accepted it, however: Ida Browne's

claims could not be tested, as documents and family memorabilia on which they were based were destroyed in a fire. All that is certain is that Blackmore drew on pre-existing stories about the Doones, Tom Faggus, and perhaps a prototype 'Jan' Ridd. What they may have been like can be gauged from an article in *Fraser's Magazine* for October 1857 where 'T' (actually the Revd George Tugwell) described walking on Exmoor 'one pleasant summer evening long ago' and encountering a peat-cutter named Jan, who entertained him with local traditions. He told of Tom Faggus and his 'enchanted strawberry horse' – always 'he' in Jan's account, not a mare as in *Lorna Doone* – ending with the sad tale (suppressed by Blackmore) of how finally the 'kind-hearted robber' was caught by a detective dressed up as a beggar, and for once the 'enchanted horse' could not save him, for at that moment he was shot dead in his stable by a 'runner' while peacefully eating his corn.

And, says 'T':

We do not forget with what seriousness he [Jan] told us of . . . the Doones of Badgeworthy, at whose name Exmoor children quake. . . . How . . . one dark night, they suddenly appeared before a lone barton or homestead . . . and burst through the frail protections of bolt and door – being aware . . . that the farmer and his servants were at work in their distant fields. But there was a little child and a servant girl remaining. The girl . . . left her charge at the first token of danger, and hid herself in the neighbouring oven. . . . The Doones being hungry . . . laid hands on the unfortunate infant, cooked him, and ate him . . . and whilst they washed down his remnants with some of his father's old ale, chanted the following refrain:

> If anyone asks who 'twas that eat thee,
> Tell them – the Doones of Badgworthy.

Dragons

A belief in monsters resembling huge serpents, often with legs and wings, can be found in the folklore of cultures far more ancient than Britain's, including the two earliest recorded mythologies, the Babylonian and the Indian. 'Dragon', the term conventionally used to translate the various names for these monsters, comes from a Greek word meaning 'large serpent'. Celts in Britain may well have known tales about dragon-slayers, but if so they were never put into writing, and the first recorded in these islands are the Germanic ones about Beowulf and Sigemund the Volsung, both featured in the Old English epic *Beowulf*.

The dragon in *Beowulf* is snake-like (it is regularly called a 'worm'); it has wings, but no legs are mentioned; its weapons are its fiery breath and its venomous bite. Its lair is a hollow, rocky burial mound on a cliff, where gold treasures had been laid as funeral offerings for some long-dead chieftain. The association between dragons, burial mounds, and buried treasure was very strong in pre-Conquest England, but barely survives in later local folklore; a few mounds have names referring to dragons, but their stories are lost.

In religious art and saints' legends, a dragon stands for Satan or demons in general; this follows Revelation 12, with its battle between the Archangel Michael and 'that old serpent called the Devil', and Mark 16:18 and Luke 10:19, where the power of Christians to overcome evil is symbolized as an ability to hold or trample on deadly snakes. In medieval hagiography there are hosts of legends about saints who overcame dragons, or cursed or banished snakes, or turned them to stone as St Hilda did at Whitby Abbey, Yorkshire. The most famous in England is, of course, St George.

In military and heraldic symbolism, however, a dragon stands for valour and menace – for instance, it was the emblem of Uther Pendragon (father of King Arthur), and appears as the heraldic device of many aristocratic families. When Sir Francis Drake was knighted by Elizabeth I, he chose to incorporate a dragon in the coat of arms granted to him, as a pun upon his own surname and an allusion to his ferocity in battle, since 'drake' is an alternative word for 'dragon'.

The dragons of local legends differ from those in myths, heroic epic, or saints' lives because they are so intimately linked to the place where the tale is told. Typically, the story will explain in minute detail where the dragon had his lair, where he hunted, and where the hero fought and killed him. Almost always it draws attention to some material object which links the amazing events of the tale to the ongoing, everyday world: a bare patch on the hillside where the dragon's blood fell; the hero's weapon, preserved by his descendants; his tomb, with or without an effigy; a painting, statue, or church carving alleged to represent the combat. These local allusions not only make the story vivid, but also constitute a claim on the hearer's belief – how could anybody doubt the dragon's reality when one can see the axe that killed him?

Rather surprisingly, the story of St George made little impact on local legends; only two places claim to be the site of his famous fight: Brinsop, Herefordshire, and Dragon Hill, Berkshire. In the vast majority of cases, the hero of a dragon-slaying legend is neither a saint, nor an anonymous knight, but someone closely identified with the place itself. There are two ways in which this can come about. Either the hero is supposed to have been a member (perhaps even the founder) of some important family of landowning aristocracy or gentry long established in the district, in which case it is often added that the family's titles, lands, and wealth were a reward for his success; often, such a family has a dragon in its coat-of-arms, popularly taken as proof of the tale, but more likely to have been its inspiration. Or the hero is presented as a working-class local lad, a farm labourer, blacksmith, soldier, or even a criminal; his name, if he has one, is suitably plebeian and may be common in the area, as 'Puttock' for the hero at Lyminster. Rewards for these men are rarely mentioned; if they are, they are more often money than land, let alone titles. It is not uncommon for the hero (whether gentry or villager) to die at the moment of triumph, poisoned by the breath or the blood of the monster he had killed – a tragic irony already present in the Beowulf story.

Tales with upper-class heroes generally give only a cursory account of the climactic battle in which the knight, relying on normal chivalric weapons, dispatches his foe; these battles conform to the norms established by the St George legend, and perhaps for that very reason do not inspire much creative invention. But there are many more where the storytellers delight in describing a victory ingeniously won through eccentric weapons and elaborate tricks, building up the details in a way which combines excitement, surprise, and humour. An element of poetic justice often adds to the enjoyment – a fire-breathing dragon choked by smoke from a smouldering peat, a greedy one laid low by food he rashly gulped down, a powerful one fatally wounded through his own strength. Whether humorous or moralistic, whether triumphant or tragic in its outcome, a tale of dragon-slaying is always fine entertainment.

Fairies

'Fairy' is a medieval word, derived from French, for a species of non-human yet material being with magical powers; they can be visible or invisible at will, change their appearance, fly (by their own power, *not* with wings), live underground or in woodland or water, grant good or bad luck to humans, cause sickness, and abduct children or adults into fairyland. An older English word for them was 'elf' (now a literary term); well-known local names include 'puck', 'pixie', 'brownie', and 'hob'. As fairies can be mischievous, indeed dangerous, there is some overlap between them and the 'boggarts' and bogeys, which were thought to pose a threat to people in lonely or dangerous places. In *A Midsummer Night's Dream*, Shakespeare's Puck, though in no way evil, boasts of tricks, shape-changing, and leading travellers astray. Beings of this nature are part of European folklore; in medieval England they were a matter for serious belief, but this gradually faded, leaving only scattered anecdotes. Some people, however, still believed these anecdotes to be true; at Kington, Herefordshire, in the early twentieth century, one woman accepted the truth of stories she had heard about a changeling, and about a girl carried into fairyland because she stepped inside a fairy ring.

Fairies can be divided into two main groups, the

'social' fairies who live in communities of their own and are occasionally seen engaged in group activities (dancing, feasting, holding markets, travelling), and the 'household' fairies, who attach themselves to a human farm or household, as helpers and luck-bringers. Brownies, hobs and pixies often take on this role. Stories about the household fairy stress that he should never be spied on or laughed at, for he will then disappear, and the farm will lose its luck; the foolish man who offended them may well be punished too, as in the story from Arlington, Sussex. Nor should a brownie be offered new clothes, or, as Reginald Scot noted in his *Discoverie of Witchcraft* (1584, Book 4, Chapter 10), he will 'chafe exceedingly' (be very annoyed) and refuse ever to work again. But household fairies can also be troublesome – in extreme cases, almost as noisy and destructive as a poltergeist. One anecdote, told in several places in northern and eastern counties, tells how a farmer was so pestered by a noisy hob that he decided to move elsewhere to escape him – only to discover the hob had hidden among the household goods, and was coming too.

Medieval sources have recorded several elaborate and colourful tales about the encounters between human beings and the world of the social fairies. There is the story of Herla, who was invited into a wonderful fairy kingdom inside a mountain, where centuries passed like days; of Edric, who took as his bride a fairy he saw dancing with her sisters in the forest of Clun, Shropshire; of St Collen, who unmasked the fairies of Glastonbury Tor, Somerset, as demons; of the fairies feasting inside Willy Howe, Yorkshire, and a mound in the Forest of

Dean, Gloucestershire, whose human guest stole their goblet. In 1684, Richard Bovet in his *Pandaemonium* wrote of a man who saw crowds of fairies holding a market on the Blackdown Hills, Somerset. In later folklore, the most common tale about a human being who actually enters fairyland is that a woman or girl is summoned there to act as midwife to a fairy woman in labour, as at Taunton, Somerset, or as nursemaid to a fairy child, as on the Lady Downs and elsewhere in Cornwall. These stories often involve the notion that the girl acquires the power to see fairies, who are normally invisible to humans, because she has put some magical ointment of theirs onto her own eye; later, she foolishly lets them realize that she has this power, and so loses it.

One widespread legend-type concerns a ploughman who overhears a fairy inside a mound who is grieving because he (or she) has broken a baking tool; the kindly ploughman mends the tool, and though he does not see the fairy he does find a delicious cake baked specially for him. Here, it is safe to eat fairy food, which gives good luck. This legend is found in Berkshire, Sussex, Somerset, and Worcestershire. At Frensham, Surrey, fairies helped humans by lending them a large cauldron, until one day some ungrateful person did not return it. Similarly, the wonderful cow of Mitchell's Fold, Shropshire, was sent by fairies, but left for ever when the gift of its milk was abused.

On the whole, English legends about fairies do not show them as malevolent, whereas water spirits, bogeys, and so on, are. Stories about changelings are found, but it seems that, at any rate in the post-medieval period, deformities and sickness in children or in farm animals were blamed on witches, not fairies. By the nineteenth and twentieth centuries, the only situation in which anyone was encouraged to take fairies seriously was when parents persuaded their children that fairies would take away their shed milk-teeth and leave money instead. This tenacious idea can be traced back to 1648, when Robert Herrick, in verses on 'Oberon's Palace' in his *Hesperides*, describes its floors as paved with 'children's teeth late shed', which, together with various other items, were 'brought thither by the elves'.

Freshwater Mermaids

It was the opinion of the Revd Robert Forby, expressed in his *Vocabulary of East Anglia* (1830), that in his time 'The . . . mermaid is only remembered as a bugbear to frighten children from the water.'

The role of 'bugbear' that Forby assigns the mermaid is not necessarily the symptom of the degradation of tradition that he implies. In fact, this is probably her most widespread function in English legends, as applicable to landlocked as to coastal counties. For just as mermaids of the sea drowned sailors, so inland mermaids lurked in rivers and ponds waiting to drown passers-by, especially children.

In Suffolk, the River Gipping was reputed to contain them. In a poem from 1837, James Bird, who was born in 1788 at Earl Stonham and died in 1839 at Yoxford, describes his own boyhood, and his mother calling out to him:

> Make haste and do your errand. Go not nigh
> The river's brink, for there the mermaids lie.
> Be home at five!

Mainly, however, mermaids lived in pits and pools. Although sharing the name 'mermaid' with the half-fish creature of the bestiaries and heraldry, they probably represent native tradition rather than learned lore. The 'mer' of mermaid is Old English *mere*, a pool, and it formed the first element of Old English *mere-wīf*, 'mere wife', the name applied in the eighth century in *Beowulf* to Grendel's mother, a cannibalistic ogress who lived beneath a lake. This lake, like many haunted pits and ponds in English folklore, is described by the poet as *grundleās*, bottomless.

The Cambridgeshire poet J. R. Withers was speaking of the countryside around Fordham when he wrote in 1864:

> And strange were the tales of the pond in the meadow,
>   And eager we listened with eyes opened wide
> To those tales often told by poor Mary the widow,
>   Who lived in a cottage the meadow beside.
> Play not, my dear boys, near the pond in the meadow,
>   The mermaid is waiting to pull you beneath;
> Climb not for a bird's nest, the bough it may sliver,
>   And the mermaid will drag you to darkness and death.

There were likewise mermaids in Suffolk pools, among them the Mermaid Pits at Fornham All Saints. A correspondent wrote in 'Suffolk Notes and Queries' in about 1877 that a well in the village (unspecified) reputedly held a mermaid, while another sent word of a mermaid at Rendlesham.

'C.W.J.' writing from Suffolk in Robert Chambers's *Book of Days* (1863–4) said that mermaids were supposed to abound in the ponds and ditches of the neighbourhood. 'I once asked a child what mermaids were, and he was ready with his answer at once, "Them nasty things what crome (*i.e.*, hook you) into the water!"' The savagery of these mermaids is echoed in a belief, said by Morley Adams in about 1914 to have been held by the 'fen-folk', that every now and then a web-footed child was born. Mostly girls, they were always beautiful, and unless their bare feet were seen it was impossible to tell them from ordinary people. But they had 'a strong homicidal tendency', and generally drowned their victims in the dykes.

The mermaids of the Eastern Counties had their counterparts in water bugbears of the North, Jinny or Jenny Greenteeth in the Lake Counties and Peg Powler of the Tees. Marjorie Rowling, in *The Folklore of the Lake District* (1979), wrote of her own belief as a child in Jinny Greenteeth. The maid, Katy Wyatt, who daily took her and her sister for a walk, told them that the monster still lived 'down the back lane' at Kirkby Lonsdale. The slimy pool which was her original home had dried up, but Katy, a local girl, assured them that she still lived in nearby Lunefield wood 'and would rush out and gobble us up if we were naughty'.

Peg Powler, for her part, had green tresses and an insatiable lust for human life. Jinny Greenteeth is sometimes explained as personifying the green scum of duckweed on stagnant water, but green tresses sound like a metaphor for green weeds waiting to entangle limbs. Marine mermaids are also often described in folktales as having long green hair.

Similar childhood bugbears were Grindylow and Nelly Long-Arms – the latter known from Yorkshire to Shropshire. Outside the nursery, too, mermaids could be sinister figures, as at Blake Mere and Chapel-en-le-Frith, Derbyshire. Sometimes they guarded treasure, as at Child's Ercall, Shropshire; or else lost bells, as at Marden, Herefordshire. Despite what Forby says, belief in them seems to have persisted even among adults into the first half of the nineteenth century, judging from an anecdote told by Augustus Hare in 1876 concerning Rostherne Mere, Cheshire.

The Gabriel Hounds

William Wordsworth (1770–1850), living in the Lake District, wrote:

> For overhead are sweeping Gabriel's Hounds,
> Doomed, with their impious lord, the flying hart
> To chase for ever on aërial grounds
>   (*Miscellaneous Sonnets*, canto 2:29)

The Gabriel's Hounds, as Robert Plot in 1686 also called them, were a mysterious phenomenon known in many parts of England. Dr Plot attributed their cry in the night, such as people had heard at Wednesbury, to wild geese. The ornithologist William Yarrell two centuries later said it was the bean goose, overwintering in Britain and noisy at night on the wing. These explanations are far in spirit from folk traditions. In his *Glossary of the Cleveland Dialect* (1868), the Revd J. C. Atkinson says that people in Cleveland linked Gabriel Hounds or Ratchets or Raches with a supernatural bird with large glowing eyes, hooked beak, and terrifying shriek, appearing to, or heard calling by, the doomed.

Most people, however, interpreted them as dogs. An informant told William Henderson in 1861 that he heard them one dark night as he was passing Sheffield parish church and the sound was 'like the questing of a dozen beagles'. Their very names bespeak canine ancestry. 'Ratchets' and 'Raches' contain Old English *ræcc*, a dog that hunts by scent. William Brockie, writing in 1886 of beliefs in and around Durham, where some people called them 'Sky Yelpers', describes them as 'monstrous human-headed dogs'. In some places they were called 'Gabble Ratchets', and 'Gabble' may be an older name, imitating their cries: in Cleveland, 'Gabriel-ratchet' was pronounced *Gaabrl-ratchet*, suggesting that in dialect they sounded much the same.

Probably a Middle English term, no longer understood, has been changed to something familiar. The medieval *Promptorium Parvulorum*, a Latin–English vocabulary, gives 'Gabriel' as a variant of *gabares*, which it equates with Latin *funus*, 'burial', 'death', and Middle English *lyche*, 'dead body'. From this, the Revd Mr Atkinson concluded that *Gabrielle rache*, recorded from 1483, 'appears to be simply *gabbares-rache* . . . corpse-hound'.

This meaning accords with later traditions: in the nineteenth century, if the Gabriel Hounds or Ratchets hovered over a house, death or calamity followed. In *Notes on the Folk-Lore of the Northern Counties* (1866), Henderson records that, when a child was burned to death in Sheffield some years previously, the neighbours immediately recalled the Gabriel Hounds passing over the house. He was also told that someone called one night to a sickbed was accompanied by them all the way, and they yelped over the house, where he found that his relative had just died.

Once assumed to contain the name 'Gabriel', the Gabriel Hounds acquired an underlying story. Most people explained the phenomenon as a spectral hunt. Sometimes its leader, Gabriel, was a man. According to Derbyshire legend at the beginning of the twentieth century, he was a squire who persisted in hunting on Sundays, once driving his pack into the church, for which sacrilege he is condemned to ride for ever on windy nights. This 'Sabbath-breaker' story was the one known to Wordsworth. Atkinson reports a Cleveland variant concerning 'a gentleman of olden times . . . so strangely fond of hunting that, on his deathbed, he ordered his hounds all to be killed and buried . . . in the same tomb as himself'. In consequence, both he and they maintain a perpetual hunt (it was sacrilege to bury animals, thought to have no souls, in consecrated ground).

Sometimes Gabriel is the Archangel. According to a Derbyshire correspondent writing to *Notes and Queries* in 1886, 'the angel Gabriel was hunting . . . [the damned] and . . . the cries were uttered as the lash of the angel's whip urged them along.' Both versions relate to tales of demonic huntsmen, like the hunting priest Dando and his Dogs at St Germans, Cornwall, carried off by the Devil for hunting on the Sabbath, though his dogs continued to be heard early on Sundays. Both, with their penitential themes, are a far cry from the tradition at Hammerwich that the sound was of angels bearing away 'blessed souls'. This may be a Victorian sentimentalization of an old tradition associating such cries with the souls of unbaptized children. In Germany, a troop of such souls was led by Berchta or Perchta, said in folk tradition to appear on the Twelve Nights of Christmas, especially on Twelfth Night.

Henderson points out the similarity between this and what was said around Leeds concerning the 'Gabble retchet': 'It was held to be the souls of unbaptised children doomed to flit restlessly around their parents' abode.' He also knew of a servant in the clergyman's family at Chudleigh, Devon, who some years before had asked if what local people said was true, 'about the souls of unchristened children wandering in the air till the Judgment Day'. Similarly the Victorian novelist Charles Reade, in *Put Yourself in His Place* (1869), set in Sheffield, has a villager say of the 'Gabble retchet', 'They are not hounds at all; they are the souls of unbaptised children.'

St Augustine (d. 430) taught that baptism was necessary to salvation and therefore unbaptized children who died went to Hell though, as innocents, they did not suffer all its pains. Medieval Catholic theologians, to mitigate the distress this caused bereaved parents, postulated the existence of Limbo, where unbaptized children enjoyed a blissful state after death, though excluded from the Beatific Vision (seeing God face to face). In parts of France, this was further mitigated by special sanctuaries where priests baptized stillborn babies, under the fiction that they still lived, enabling them to be buried in consecrated ground and enter Heaven. Perhaps the harsh character of early Protestantism explains why the punitive concept of tiny wandering souls survived in England without amelioration.

Giants

Giants have two main roles in local legends: as creators of landscape features which appear to be artificial yet are beyond the strength of ordinary men, and as the butt of jokes about their foolishness. Often, both roles are combined, as in the famous tale of The Wrekin. The greatest concentration of such legends are found in mountainous areas, especially Cumberland, Westmorland, and Cornwall. Speaking of Cornwall, J. T. Blight wrote in 1861:

. . . it is the tradition of the country that a much larger race of men stalked over this ground than any that are now to be seen . . . By the vibrations of their laughter and shouts great fissures were shaken in the cliffs . . . they left their footprints in the solid rock . . . They do not appear to have been wicked . . . their chief business seems to have been to throw about and overturn huge rocks.

Some Cornish giants had names, like Bolster of Bolster Bank, John of Gaunt of Carn Brea Castle, Jack of Giant's Hedge, Wrath or Ralph of Ralph's Cupboard, and Dan Dynas of Treryn Dinas. However, most were anonymous. Theoretically, giants are enemies to humanity, though their hostile plans are always thwarted through their own clumsiness or stupidity. Some medieval legends did present them as a threat, notably Geoffrey of Monmouth's account of the defeat of Gogmagog. Later, legends about them were not taken seriously, unlike those about fairies; the only evidence of belief in their continued existence comes from Cornwall and the Scilly Isles in the eighteenth century. There, in 1752, the antiquary William Borlase was excavating certain prehistoric burial cairns of a type popularly called 'Giants' Graves' when a violent storm occurred. Next day, people were complaining that their crops were ruined, and one woman asked 'whether I did not think that we had disturbed the giants, and said that many good people . . . were of opinion that the giants were offended, and had really raised that storm'. As giants were well known to possess treasure, he was also asked how much money he had found in the graves.

There are 'Giant's Caves' in various districts, sometimes named after their reputed owner, for example, 'Samson the giant's chamber' at Lazonby, Cumberland; 'Giant's Grave' is another common name, applied to barrows and earthworks. Giants are also repeatedly associated with large isolated boulders and prehistoric standing stones, which they are alleged to have dropped or flung from a great distance. Sometimes they carried stones for some building project, but dropped them; they did, however, complete one spectacular structure, Wade's Causeway in North Yorkshire. Other giants hurled rocks at one another as weapons (Wilmington, Sussex); or competed to see who could throw furthest (Melcombe Horsey, Dorset). In Cornwall their favourite game, wrote James Orchard Halliwell-Phillipps in 1861, 'consisted in throwing granite boulders ... as a quoit, formed of pillars of stone surmounted with a large one laid flat on their top, placed in a conspicuous position on the summit or brow of a hill' – i.e. a Neolithic or early Bronze Age burial chamber, the covering mound of which has weathered away or been ploughed out. Such monuments, called 'the Giant's Quoit', are at Lanyon, Mulfra, Pawton, Trethevy, and Zennor (all in Cornwall).

Sometimes two giants, jointly owning a single hammer, would toss it to one another as required, as at Consett, Co. Durham, and Putney, London; the results could be fatal, as at Trencrom Castle, Cornwall. In such stories, however, there is no reference to the landscape.

Besides these wholly superhuman giants, there are several human folk heroes who are credited with gigantic stature or strength, at least in some of the tales about them. Thus, in Herefordshire King Arthur lifted the capstone of a megalithic tomb, Robin Hood's Butts were clods of earth that fell from his shoes as he and Little John competed in mighty leaps, and Jack O'Kent could hurl boulders further than the Devil. Particularly interesting are the legends where a large grave, or an arrangement of stones taken to be such, is said to prove the exceptional size of some local hero. Notable examples are Tom Hickathrift at Tilney All Saints, Norfolk; Jack of Legs at Weston, Hertfordshire; Little John at Hathersage, Derbyshire; Sir Hugh Cesario at Penrith, Cumberland; and Sir John Talbot at Whitwick, Leicestershire.

Gogmagog

The London Guildhall contains statues of the giants Gog and Magog, the latest in a series of effigies which can be traced back for over 300 years, originally under the names of Gogmagog and Corineus. They are the guardians of the city and symbols of patriotic pride. This is clearly seen in a charming miniature book produced in 1741 by a printer named Thomas Boreman. It consists of two tiny volumes, grandly entitled *The Gigantick History of the Two Famous Giants of Guildhall:*

Corineus and Gogmagog were two brave giants, who nicely [scrupulously] valued their honour, and exerted their whole strength and force in defence of their liberty and country; so the City of London, by placing these their representatives in their Guildhall, emblematically declare that they will, like mighty giants, defend the honour of their country, and the liberty of this their city, which excels all others as much as those huge giants exceed in stature the common bulk of mankind.

But this was not always so; Gogmagog began his career as an archetypal ogre, and Corineus as his adversary. Geoffrey of Monmouth's *History of the Kings of Britain* (*c.*1136) claims that when Brutus of Troy reached Britain it was inhabited by giants, whom he drove away into remote mountain regions. His follower Corineus went to Cornwall because 'naught gave him greater pleasure than to wrestle with the giants, of whom there was greater plenty there than in any of the other provinces'. There, one particularly ferocious giant named Goemagot led a surprise attack on Brutus's men while they were at a feast, and slew many before being defeated. He was captured, but not put to death; instead, a wrestling match was arranged between him and Corineus, who eventually hoisted the giant onto his shoulders and hurled him over a cliff onto the rocks below, where he died. The place was still called Goemagot's Leap in Geoffrey's time, and is traditionally said to be Plymouth Hoe.

Geoffrey's book exists in two versions, one in Latin and one in Norman French, which accounts for the giant's curious name – a phonetic rendering of French *Got et Magot* (the t's are silent), the French names for the mysterious biblical figures referred to in English as Gog and Magog. In Ezekiel 38–9 it is prophesied that 'Gog from the land of Magog' will attack Israel; in Revelations 20 both names refer to powerful supporters of Antichrist. Medieval interpreters sometimes ran both words together as a single name, Gogmagog, for a supremely evil giant.

In the Middle Ages, the people of Plymouth carved the figure of a giant on the slopes of the Hoe. The account books of Plymouth Corporation between 1486 and 1566 show periodic payments for cleaning 'the Gogmagog'. At some point a second figure must have been made, for Richard Carew's *Survey of Cornwall* (1602) states:

Moreover upon the Haw at Plymouth there is cut in the ground the portrayture of two men, the one bigger, the other lesser, with clubbes in their hands (whom they terme *Gog Magog*), and (as I have learned) it is renewed by order of the townsmen when cause requireth, which would infer the same to be a monument of some moment.

A few years later, however, the smaller figure was being called Corineus. The site was destroyed when the Citadel was built in the reign of Charles I. There is a mild discrepancy between Geoffrey's narrative and the Plymouth hill figures, in that the former describes a wrestling match, whereas the latter are armed with clubs, as at Cerne Abbas, Dorset. This is almost certainly due to the influence of heraldry and pageantry, where it was conventional to represent a Wild Man as large, half naked, and wielding a crude club.

A new version of Geoffrey of Monmouth's story evolved in Tudor times, asserting that Brutus captured Gog and Magog alive and brought them to London to be porters at the gates of his palace. London, like many other cities, frequently used effigies of giants in civic pageantry. A male and female pair greeted Henry V on London Bridge as he entered in triumph in 1415; a Gogmagog and a Corineus welcomed Mary Tudor and Philip of Spain in 1554, and Elizabeth in 1559. Such giants were periodically paraded at Lord Mayors' pageants and Midsummer Shows over the next three centuries, and between whiles were often displayed in the Guildhall; sometimes they were called Samson and Hercules, sometimes Gogmagog and Corineus, eventually 'Gog and

Magog'. Children were amazed to be told that 'every day, when the giants hear the clock strike twelve, they come down to dinner.'

Those meant for processions were generally made of wickerwork and moved by men walking inside them. Alternatives were possible too – in 1605, for example, they were impersonated by stilt-walkers, and in 1672 a huge pair, fifteen feet (4.6 m) tall, sat in chariots, 'moving, talking, and taking tobacco as they ride along'. Some came to sad ends: one pair was destroyed during the Commonwealth; their successors were lost in the Great Fire of London; another pair fell victim to rats. In 1708, a very fine pair was carved in wood; these, being too heavy to move, remained permanently in the Guildhall, and lightweight wicker replicas were provided for pageants. On 9 November 1827, when the latter were paraded again after many years of neglect, they 'appeared to call forth more admiration and applause than fell to the share of any of the other personages who formed part of the Procession' (*The Times*, 10 November 1827). Sadly, the wooden figures perished in the Blitz in 1940. The pair currently displayed was made in 1953 for the Festival of Britain.

Hangman's Stones

Many local legends are underpinned by a strong communal sense of morality. Among these are tales where crime meets an unexpected and dramatic punishment, which may be either horrifying or grimly amusing. There are over two dozen places in England and Wales where there is (or used to be) a large boulder, milestone, or mounting block locally known as the Hangman's Stone, or a stile or gate called Gallows Gate; in each place, the story told to account for the name is virtually the same.

A fine example of the type is given by Bob Copper, the well-known Sussex folk singer, in his book *A Song for Every Season* (1975); his father Jim Copper had told it to him when he was a child, having learned it in turn from his own father. It concerns a large boulder, some three feet (0.9 m) high, which stands near the cliff edge at Rottingdean.

It seems there was once a rogue from Brighton who stole a sheep from a farm in Saltdean, and decided it would be less trouble to lead the live animal home on a rope than to kill it and carry it for about three miles (5 km). By the time he got as far as Rottingdean, night was falling and he was thirsty, so he tethered the sheep to the boulder and went down into the village for a drink. However, he stayed so long in the pub and drank so much that when at last he staggered back to the cliff path all he wanted to do was to rest a while, and he sat down with his back propped against the same boulder as the sheep was tied to. He fell fast asleep – and never woke again. As Copper explains:

The red light of dawn revealed a gruesome scene. The sheep was grazing contentedly on the green cliff turf, but on the other end of its tethering rope the sheep-stealer lay strangled. In those days his crime of sheep stealing was punishable by death, and the little drama had been played out to the end. The crime had been committed, the criminal apprehended, so to speak, found guilty, sentenced, and despatched all in one act.

To appreciate the full implications of the tale, one should realize that sheep rearing was vital to the economic success of Sussex Downland farms, so that sheep-stealing would be seen as a very serious threat. It is no accident that the thief in this story is said to be a Brighton man, for that town's reputation for harbouring crooks goes back a very long way.

The same story can be found in Northumberland. It is told of a boulder somewhere near the village of Catton in Allendale, not now identifiable, which was called the Wedderstone (a wether is a castrated ram); a local couplet made the moral explicit, warning would-be sheep-stealers:

> When ye lang for a mutton bone
> Think on the Wedderstone.

For centuries, it had been the law that theft of goods above a certain value could be punished by death, and a full-grown sheep would certainly be worth enough to fall within that definition; sheep-stealing became an increasing problem in the eighteenth century, and in 1741 an Act of Parliament was passed 'to render the laws more effective for the preventing of the stealing and destroying of sheep' by making this specifically a hanging offence. In practice, however, judges who had passed sentence of death would then often commute it to transportation for several years, or for life. Eventually, in 1832, the death penalty for this form of theft was abolished. The ironic humour of the Hangman's Stone story depends on the fact that the punishment so precisely fits the crime; it may well be that the softening of the law in 1832 gave an impetus to the popularity of the tale among those who thought the thieves were now getting off too lightly. It cannot, however, be argued that this was its actual origin, since the first reference to it, at Coombe Martin, Devon, is found as early as Thomas Westcote's *A View of Devonshire in 1630*. It is probably also relevant, as Leslie Grinsell pointed out, that many of the boulders in question stand near crossroads or parish boundaries, which are common sites for gallows and gibbets.

Outside the main areas of sheep farming, one occasionally finds variants where another animal is substituted. At Shepshed, Leicestershire, on the edge of Charnwood Forest, it was said that a poacher called John of Oxley was throttled in the same way by the body of a stolen deer. In Condover Park, Shropshire, the animal concerned is said to have been a hare, though this led only to capture, not death.

The possibility that a sheep-stealer really did die in such a way somewhere, sometime, cannot be logically ruled out. Leslie Grinsell suggested that the news could have been carried from place to place by travellers, turning into a story which could be repeatedly relocated, acquiring appropriate details to fit its new site. However, as with today's contemporary 'urban legends', it is impossible to pinpoint an original site, and the plot looks suspiciously neat; one should be willing to credit oral storytellers with creative abilities.

Haunted Mines

The dangers of mining – from pit-falls to fire damp – are reflected in the beliefs of miners, especially those concerning various spirits formerly said to haunt mines. One usually appearing as a blue flame was immensely strong, and helped miners in their work if rewarded. However, if not properly treated, he brought disaster on the mine. In Northumberland, where he was known as Blue Cap or Blue Bonnet, he long haunted Shilbottle Mine, and was a hard worker, but fussy over his wages.

Quite different was Gathon, who tormented miners with noises, illusory flames, and false lights. According to William Jones in *Credulities* (1880), he or one of his kind had frightened three miners in the South Devon Wharf Mine a few years previously. They had been working one Saturday night, when suddenly they saw a large fireball issuing from a rock. As it drew close, it took on different forms, sometimes like a human figure, sometimes like a church. The men now realized that Sunday had begun, and were convinced that they were being punished as Sabbath-breakers.

One dangerous Northumbrian spirit was known as 'Cutty Soams' from the delight he took in cutting the rope traces or 'soams' by which the little assistant putters (boys and girls) were yoked to the coal-tub. An account of him in the *Colliery Guardian* in 1863 says that it was not uncommon for the men to go down to work and find that he had been busy overnight cutting every pair of traces to pieces. The only good he ever did was in a roundabout way. At Callington Pit, when an overseer called Nelson, suspected of causing the deaths of two miners, was killed by fire-damp, local rumour said it was a punishment. This was seemingly put down to Cutty Soams, and Cutty Soams Colliery, as the pit came to be known, never worked another day.

By many miners, Cutty Soams was said to be the ghost of a miner who had been killed in the pit and returned to warn his 'marrows' (workmates) of impending misfortune. If so, he was not the only revenant to haunt a mine – celebrated in West Country lore is Dorcas, of Polbreen Mine, St Agnes, Cornwall. Nor was Cutty Soams the only ominous spectre encountered: the lead miners of Derbyshire feared appearances of a ghostly black dog that prowled round old mines, while Robert Hunt in *Popular Romances of the West of England* (1881) records that, at Wheal Vor, Cornwall, it had always been believed that a fatal accident in the mine was presaged by a hare or white rabbit in one of the engine-houses: 'The men solemnly declare that they have chased these appearances . . . without being able to catch them.' The *Colliery Guardian* of 23 May 1863 likewise spoke of 'a little white animal like a rabbit', which, if it crossed the miners' path, was a warning not to go down the pit.

Some mines were haunted by knockers, diminutive miners like German kobolds, and so-called from the sounds of their working. In the tin mines of Cornwall, where they were also known as *buccas* (a name related to Puck), they were explained as the 'sperrits' of the Jews condemned to the mines as a penance for their part in the Crucifixion, or as the last of an ancient race that once lived in Cornwall and, being neither good enough for Heaven nor bad enough for Hell, was doomed to remain forever earthbound. A famous haunt of theirs was the Ballowal Mine, close to Ballowal Barrow, near St Just.

The knockers were ambiguous creatures: some thought it good luck to hear them because they only worked rich lodes of tin; thus leading the miners to them; others took the sound as an omen of disaster, often (as in reality) presaging a pit-fall. Like Gathon, they were believed to enforce traditional mining customs, notably the ban on work on certain holy days. A correspondent of *Notes and Queries* in 1855 comments on the 'almost universal aversion' miners had to entering a mine on Good Friday, Holy Innocents' Day (28 December), or Christmas Day, and says that, when he visited one of the lead mines in Allendale, Northumberland, he found that, rather than work on those days, miners would sacrifice their employment. When asked why, they explained that some catastrophe would befall them if they defied custom.

Knockers were easily offended, as a miner called 'Barker' from Towednack, Cornwall, found out. Barker heard them talking and learned that, coming off shift, they hid their tools. Planning to steal them, he pricked up his ears when one said, 'I'll leave mine in a cleft', and another said, 'I'll leave mine under the ferns.' But the third said, 'And I'll leave mine on Barker's knee.' Suddenly Barker felt a great blow and to his dying day he walked with a limp – hence the Cornish saying 'As stiff as Barker's knee'.

Hobs, Hobthrusts and Hobmen

Hobs, hobthrusts, hobmen, and indeed hobbits (a name not invented by J. R. R. Tolkien but recorded in the nineteenth century) were spirits found mostly in the North and North Midlands and not clearly distinguished from boggarts and brownies.

In his *Glossary of the Cleveland Dialect* (1868), the Revd J. C. Atkinson says, 'Probably, there were many Hobs, each with a "local habitation" and a "local name." ' A few had personal names, such as Hodge Hob o'Bransdale, Robin Round-cap of Spaldington, Old Delph Will of Saddleworth, and Elphi Bandy Legs of Low Farndale, all in Yorkshire. Most, however, were called simply 'Hob'. A list of hobmen in the Pickering district, Yorkshire, from 1823 includes Lealholm Hob, Scugdale Hob, T' Hob o' Brakken Howe, and Hob o' Hasty Bank. Most hobs are male, though we hear of a hobthrust mother at Irstones, Staffordshire, who stole a baby and left a 'changeling' in its place. Francis Grose, in his *Provincial Glossary* (1787), explains 'hobthrust' as being properly 'hob o't'hurst . . . supposed to haunt woods only.' Philologists prefer to derive it from Old English *thyrs*, later *thurse*, a giant.

Although there is no indication that hobs and hobthrusts were giant-size, they often shared the same habitat as the thurse. Bishop White Kennett in a glossary of the Lancashire dialect, written *c*.1700, defines 'Thurs-house or Thurs-hole' as 'a hollow vault in a rock or stony hill . . . looked on as enchanted holes'. Hobs and hobthrusts are similarly associated in English place-names both with natural caverns as at Breedon and Hob Hole, Runswick Bay, Yorkshire, and with artificial 'caves' or tumuli like Obtrusch Roque, Farndale, Yorkshire, and Hob Hurst's House, Beeley, Derbyshire. Some hobs were thought to haunt fields and more particularly transitional places, which traditionally always attracted spirits: Fletcher Moss, in *Folk-Lore: Old Customs and Tales of my Neighbours* (1898), notes not only a Hob Croft, but also a Hob Lane and a Hob Bridge at Gatley, Lancashire.

Hobs and hobthrusts were mixed in character. In Yorkshire, notable hob territory, they included spirits who 'lived in' and did household chores, like the hobs of Hart Hall in Glaisdale, and Hob Hill, Upleatham; and some who, like the hobman of Marske-by-the-Sea, lived outside human society but safeguarded the community. The hob of Breedon on the Hill, Leicestershire, lived in a household but when offended turned feral and went to live by himself in a cave. Similarly the hob of Silton in the Vale of Mowbray left home when not given his usual reward of bread and butter, and went to live in a cave called after him Hobthrush Hall. Some wild hobs terrorized their neighbourhoods and were dealt with like bogeys and ghosts: Hob Hedeless (Headless), of Hurworth, Co. Durham, was 'laid' under a boulder for ninety-nine years and a day.

One of the most popular stories attached to house-dwelling hobs is the gift of clothes. Such spirits were traditionally naked, and in 1584 Reginald Scot wrote of one of the more famous, Robin Goodfellow:

... he would chafe exceedingly, if the maid or goodwife of the house, having compassion of his nakednes, laid anie clothes for him ... For in that case he saith; What haue we here? Hemton, hamten, here will I neuer more tread nor stampen.

From similar rhymes in later stories, it appears that the spirit is displeased with a hempen garment, made of material like sacking, the common dress of labourers.

This theme goes back to medieval demonology: the fourteenth-century Dominican preacher John of Bromyard tells of a *diabolus* who was given clothes as a reward for his labours and immediately downed tools, 'saying in English "Now I have a cape and a hood, I will do no more good"'. Another medieval author speaks of a demon who, on being given a new tunic, remarks before vanishing, 'suld syche a proude grome [fellow] grynd corn?' The hobs of later English folklore react to the clothes in the same ways: they resent the attempt to clothe them, or they are dissatisfied with the garment, or they feel too gentrified to work. The outcome is the same: they leave, like the hobs of Sturfit Hall, near Reeth, and Close House, Skipton-in-Craven, Yorkshire; Manor Farm, East Halton, Lincolnshire; and Elsdon Moat, Co. Durham.

A contrasting story was 'Ay, we're flitting', about a spirit whose 'family' tries to 'flit' (move house) to get away from him, but he goes too. It was told among others of Robin Round-cap and of a bogle named Jesse at West Land Ends farm, Northumberland, in the 1870s. The poet laureate Alfred, Lord Tennyson, heard it in Lincolnshire and retold it in 'Walking to the Mail' (1842), but the liveliest version appeared in the *Literary Gazette* in 1825, concerning a Yorkshire farmer called George Gilbertson and a mischievous boggart. Finally they reached an understanding, and the children would push a shoehorn through a knothole in panelling, for the boggart to push it back, in a game they called 'laking wi' t' Boggart' ('playing with Boggart').

King Arthur

Whether there was a real Arthur in the sixth century is probably an unanswerable question. The first glimpse of him comes in a ninth-century chronicle, *Historia Britonum*, attributed to Nennius, which simply says that 'Arthur, leader of the Britons' won twelve victories against the Saxons. To the Celts of Wales, Cornwall, and Brittany in the tenth and eleventh centuries, he was a king, whose chief warriors were Gawain, Kay, and Bedevere, and whose wife was Guinevere; there were tales of his warfare and supernatural adventures, now known only through allusions. He was killed in battle against 'Medraut' (=Mordred?), but his grave was unknown; some said he would return.

A fashion for Arthurian romances in verse (probably inspired by Breton models) arose among aristocrats in twelfth-century France and soon reached England. They envisaged Arthur's kingdom in terms familiar to their own times, including features such as knights, tournaments, and courtly love, alongside magical adventures. The love stories of Lancelot and Guinevere and of Tristan and Iseult appear at this stage, as does Percival's Grail Quest, but little is said about Arthur himself.

In the same period came the *History of the Kings of Britain* by Geoffrey of Monmouth (*c*.1136), accepted as historically reliable until well into the sixteenth century.

Here, the standard outline of Arthur's life emerges. Arthur is the son of King Uther Pendragon, begotten adulterously with magic help from Merlin, and crowned at fifteen when Uther dies; after defeating the Saxons he marries Guinevere; then he invades Europe to attack Rome, but has to return because his nephew Mordred has rebelled and captured Guinevere. He kills Mordred in battle, but is wounded himself.

Geoffrey is responsible for linking Merlin, previously an independent figure, with Arthur's story; he does not, however, include the idea that Mordred is Arthur's incestuously begotten son, nor does he include the sword in the stone and Excalibur, nor the Round Table – features which later developed in the mass of medieval Arthurian romances. All these sources were eventually united in Malory's *Le Morte D'Arthur* (1470), which gave the legend its definitive shape.

Did Arthur die? If not, where was he? Significantly, in 1113 a fight broke out at Bodmin, Cornwall, because some French clerics laughed at the locals for claiming that Arthur was still living; clearly, the belief in his possible return existed at popular level even before the outpouring of upper-class literature about him had begun. Geoffrey wrote that though gravely wounded in his final battle against Mordred at 'Camlann', Arthur was taken by boat to the island paradise of Avalon, where nine queens would heal him; where this may be, he does not say. Other medieval English authors record a belief that Arthur would 'come again to his kingdom', or 'would yet come to help the English'; Gervase of Tilbury writes (*c.*1212) that he is in a cavern in Mount Etna –

which is no compliment, as Etna was regarded as an entrance to Hell. The monks of Glastonbury Abbey, Somerset, claimed to have found the skeletons of Arthur and Guinevere in 1191. Malory must have known about this, but does not mention it; instead, he presents a variety of opinions from both written and oral sources:

No more of the very certainty of his death I never read, but thus was he led away in a ship wherein were three queens . . . [These queens later brought a corpse to a hermit near Glastonbury for burial] but yet the hermit knew not in certain that it was verily the body of King Arthur . . . Yet some men say in many parts of England that Arthur is not dead, but had by the will of Our Lord Jesu into another place, and men say that he shall come again, and he shall win the Holy Cross. I will not say it shall be so, but rather I will say, here in this world he changed his life. But many men say that there is written upon his tomb this verse: *Hic jacet Arthurus, Rex quondam Rexque futurus* ['Here lies Arthur, former King and future King'].

Local legends, however, claim that Arthur is sleeping inside a hill, but will arise and help his country in its hour of need. In several places, including Sewingshields, Northumberland, and Richmond Castle, Yorkshire, it is said that a man finds a secret doorway in a hillside, leading to a cavern where Arthur and his knights sleep, surrounded by weapons and treasures, which may include some especially significant objects, such as a sword, a horn, or a bell. At this point, confused by the situation, or forgetting instructions previously received, he handles the objects wrongly. The sleepers begin to stir, and the intruder panics and flees. He has lost his opportunity, and can never find the hidden entrance again; meanwhile, Arthur and the knights return to their enchanted sleep, for the time for their return has not yet come. Other stories, collected in the late nineteenth century, say Arthur and his court dwell inside the hill-fort of Cadbury Castle, Somerset; on the nights of the full moon they emerge on horses shod with silver.

Arthur's name occurs quite frequently in folk traditions about standing stones, earthworks, or natural rock formations, for example, Arthur's Chair and Oven in Cornwall. Other stories have him killing some local giant, as at Arthur's Stone, Herefordshire; or himself behaving like a giant when flinging rocks about at Sewingshields.

King Leir

The story of Leir, the legendary founder of Leicester, was told centuries before Shakespeare wrote *King Lear*. It appears first in Geoffrey of Monmouth's *History of the Kings of Britain* (*c.*1135), one of the most popular books of the Middle Ages, and later others translated it from Geoffrey's Latin or retold it over and over again: Fabian in his *Chronicle* (1516), William Warner in *Albion's England* (1586), Edmund Spenser in *The Faerie Queene* (1590–6). Shakespeare's main source was another play, *The True Chronicle Historie of King Leir and his Three Daughters*, published in 1605, but performed on stage in 1594 or earlier. However, he also knew it from Holinshed's *Chronicles* (1577), which said that, after the death of his father, Bladud of Bath, Somerset:

Leir was admitted ruler ouer the Britaines, in the yeare of the world 3105 . . . gouerning his land and subjects in great wealth. He made the towne of Caerleir now called Leicester . . . It is written that he had by his wife three daughters . . . whose names were Gonorilla, Regan, and Cordeilla, which daughters he greatly loued, but specially Cordeilla the youngest farre aboue the two elder.

When he was very old, Leir wished to find out which of his daughters most loved him and bequeath her the largest share of his kingdom. Gonorilla and Regan both swore that they loved him more than life, but Cordeilla replied, 'I . . . will continuallie (while I liue) loue you as my naturall father. And if you would more vnderstand of the loue that I beare you, assertaine your selfe, that so much as you haue, so much you are woorth, and so much I loue you, and no more.'

He could not understand this riddling answer and, though Cordeilla was speaking of the qualities for which she loved him, took her to mean that she valued him only for his wealth. Furious, he married off Gonorilla and Regan to the Dukes of Cornwall and Albany respectively, promising to leave each of them half his kingdom. When one of the twelve princes of Gallia (Gaul), having heard of Cordeilla's beauty, asked for her hand, Leir packed her off without a dowry to France.

As in Shakespeare's play, not many years had passed before Gonorilla and Regan had stripped the old king of his followers and he realized his mistake. He made his way to France, where Cordeilla welcomed him with joy. Her husband provided him with an army and he won back his throne. Three years later, however, he died, as did Cordeilla's husband, and she was left alone. She ruled Britain for five years, but then her nephews rebelled and threw her into prison, where she took her own life.

The flurry of literary activity surrounding this story in the sixteenth century was the result of a fashion for the legendary history of Britain, drawn mainly from Geoffrey. It was born of a need to flatter powerful patrons by publicizing the so-called 'Tudor myth' of British ancestry, promulgated by the Tudor dynasty since

Henry VII to bolster their shaky claim to the throne. From this fashion also sprang the plays *Locrine* and *Gorbuduc*, Shakespeare's *Cymbeline*, and effigies of the characters of Geoffrey's *History* for use in pageants, including the London Guildhall's Corineus and Gogmagog, and Gurgunt at Norwich Castle, Norfolk.

It also influenced antiquaries, followed by county historians, and resulted in the naming of such sites as Cymbeline's Castle, Buckinghamshire, King Lud's Intrenchments, and others. But the connection of Leir with Leicester is older, perhaps made by Geoffrey himself. There is no trace of the legend before Geoffrey tells it, though the name 'Leir' might come from the Welsh Llyr, father of Branwen and Bendigeidfran, whose stories are told in the late fourteenth-century *Red Book of Hergest*. It is possible that Geoffrey or a predecessor took a folktale and gave it the seeming of history, for the plot is shared by a group of European and Indian tales concerning ungrateful children. The Leir story itself exists in at least twenty-six variants, one of which concerns King Ine of the West Saxons, whose youngest daughter says she loves him as a father, but might come to love another (meaning a husband) better. In other tales, when her father asks how much she loves him, the princess answers 'like salt', and he assumes she holds him cheap, forgetting that salt is essential to life.

Geoffrey or another evidently then anchored this floating story to a particular spot by linking 'Leir' with 'Leicester' by false etymology, then slipped in a piece of local colour to give credibility to the tale. In Geoffrey's *History*, after the defeat of her sisters and her father's death, Cordeilla 'buried her Father in a certain underground chamber which had bidden be made under the river Soar at Leicester'. Evidently Geoffrey or the earlier storyteller had got wind of some buried structure found among Leicester's Roman remains.

The belief that Leir was buried at Leicester survived (after a fashion) into the eighteenth century. In his *History . . . of Leicestershire* (1795–1811), John Nichols says of New Park, 'There is in the Park a cave, digged out of the rock, where it is said king Leyer did hide himself from his enemies – *a cowardly part!*'

Lady Godiva

In real life, Godiva, wife of Earl Leofric of Mercia, was famous for her piety; she built a church near Evesham and founded an abbey in Coventry. Her date of birth is unknown, but she died in 1057. The story of her naked ride is first recorded by two monks of St Albans Abbey, Roger of Wendover in the twelfth century and Matthew Paris in the thirteenth; they present it as an act of courage, humility, and generosity, undertaken in response to an unreasonable demand by a tyrannical husband. The people of Coventry, they explain, were burdened by a heavy tax, so, in the words of Roger of Wendover in his *Flores Historiarum* (1235):

The saintly countess . . . often besought the earl, her husband, with earnest prayers, to free the town, by the guidance of the Holy Trinity and of the Holy Mother of God, from this slavery. The earl upbraided her for vainly seeking something so injurious to him and repeatedly forbade her to approach him again on the subject. Nevertheless in her female pertinacity she exasperated her husband with her unceasing request, and extorted from him the following reply: 'Mount your horse naked,' he said, 'and ride through the market place of the town from one side right to the other while people are gathered there, and when you return you shall claim what you desire.' And the countess answered: 'And if I wish to do this, will you give me your permission?' And the earl said: 'I will.'

Then the countess Godiva, beloved of God, on a certain day, as it is said, mounting her horse naked, loosed her hair from its bands, and her whole body was veiled, except for her fair white legs. Her journey done, unseen by a soul, she returned rejoicing to her husband, who accounted it a miracle. Then Earl Leofric granted a charter freeing the city of Coventry from its servitude and confirmed it with his seal.

There is now no way of discovering what historical event lies behind this tale. Godiva, being Lady of Coventry in her own right, could have freed the town from most taxes herself; however, there were some which only Leofric, as King Cnut's deputy, had the authority to remit. The story Roger tells shows influence both from saints' legends and from folklore. The contrast between a pious, charitable woman and her harsh husband is found, for example, in the life of St Elizabeth of Hungary, while several female saints have their chastity or modesty miraculously protected; Mary Magdalene and Mary of Egypt, both much revered in the Middle Ages, supposedly lived naked as hermits in the desert, protected from prying eyes by long, thick hair. But Godiva's hair also finds parallels in folktales in which a woman fulfils the apparently impossible challenge to appear 'neither naked nor clad' by arriving draped in her own hair, while the ordeal of a generous woman is the theme of stories at St Briavels, Gloucestershire, and Tichborne, Hampshire.

Later versions of Godiva's story, beginning with the

Chronicle of England by Richard Grafton in 1569, switch the emphasis from holiness to cleverness: she asked the magistrates to make everyone stay indoors with closed windows, so as she galloped through the town people heard the hoof-beats but did not see her.

By 1659, a new character had appeared: Peeping Tom, who opened a window to see Godiva riding by, and was struck blind. In that year, a visitor to Coventry was shown a statue of a man who had been blinded thus; this is probably the same life-size wooden figure of a man in Tudor armour, with damaged eyes, as has long been cherished as a city mascot, and is now in the Cathedral Lane Shopping Centre. It is said to date from about 1500. The Herbert Art Gallery and Museum in Coventry holds a painting of Godiva's ride, done in the Flemish style, and dated 1586; when it was cleaned in 1978, a small figure could be dimly seen looking from the window of a building in the background. If this is indeed meant to be Tom, his place in the story must go back to the sixteenth century, not the seventeenth.

The legend of Godiva has been kept vivid in pageantry. Since Elizabethan times, Coventry has held a civic procession at Midsummer, suppressed during the Commonwealth but lavishly revived under Charles II. From 1678, 'Lady Godiva' appears fairly regularly; at first the role was taken by a boy, but from 1765, when there was a real woman (fully dressed) on a white horse, she became the star attraction. In the same year, the wooden Peeping Tom was paraded too, as it was in several subsequent years; on other occasions it was displayed in the window of an inn overlooking the processional route.

In the early nineteenth century, Tom was represented in the pageant by a man inside a 'house' mounted on a wagon, who poked his head out of the window and amused the crowd by his comments. But, later in the same century, a commentator noted that this had not been done for years, 'the last poor fellow that was drawn about the town being taken ill immediately on his coming out of the house, and dying very soon after in a most shocking manner'. This may or may not be true: when a well-loved custom is discontinued, a story of some disaster is sometimes told to explain its cessation. The ribald humour of the occasion drew Victorian disapproval, but parades continued intermittently till the 1960s, and were revived in 1996.

The Lantern Man

'The Lantern Man' is a name given in east Norfolk to the ignis fatuus, a modern Latin name, recorded from 1563, meaning 'foolish fire' from its habit of flitting erratically from place to place. Ignes fatui are phosphorescent lights formerly seen in marshes and supposedly due to the spontaneous combustion of 'marsh gas' (phosphuretted hydrogen).

In the eighteenth century, around Syleham, Suffolk, they were called 'Syleham lamps', later 'Syleham lights'; and in the Norfolk Breckland known as 'Shiner' or 'the Shiners'. More often, the phenomenon was known by a personal name, such as Jack o' Lantern, Will o' the Wisp, Hobby-lanthorn, and Jenny Burnt Arse. This habit of personifying the light goes back at least to the sixteenth century. 'Kit with the Canstick' (candlestick) appears in a list of hobgoblins given by Reginald Scot in his *Discoverie of Witchcraft* (1584). Such names are based on the image of someone carrying a lighted torch, rushlight, candlestick, or lantern.

The ignis fatuus was long thought of as a malevolent being, just as Milton defined it in *Paradise Lost*:

> A wand'ring fire . . .
> Which oft, they say, some Evil Spirit attends,
> Hovering and blazing with delusive Light,

> Misleads th'amaz'd Night-Wandr'er from his way
> To bogs and mires, and oft through Pond or Pool,
> There swallowe'd up and lost . . .

According to the Revd Robert Forby, in 1830, the East Anglian term for this was 'led-will', possibly a mistake for 'will led', as someone writing to *Notes and Queries* in 1855 noted:

When about ten years old, I remember one Winsen, our old washerwoman . . . relating a circumstance that happened to her that morning. The distance from her house to my father's was about half a mile, and in a meadow, across which the footpath lays, is a hollow place . . . She stated that each time she attempted to cross this place she was irresistibly . . . prevented . . . or, as she said, was 'Will led,' . . .

Gervase of Tilbury in the thirteenth century had credited the Portunes, who looked like little old men, with this trick. If they encountered a man riding along at night, they would lead his horse by the bridle into a pond, then make off with a loud guffaw. In the Midlands, this was later called being 'Pouk-ledden', 'Puck-led'.

In medieval times, 'Pouk' was a name for the Devil, and the Norfolk Lantern Man retained this diabolic character. He both led people astray, sometimes to their deaths, and was given to violence. He objected to anyone else carrying a lantern and always 'ran to the light'. Reporting the beliefs of an old Irstead woman, Mrs Lubbock, in 1849, the Revd John Gunn said, 'she affirms, that "if any one were walking along the road with a lantern . . . Jack would come against it and dash it to pieces".' The Norfolk antiquary Walter Rye said in the 1870s that he had heard of a man who set his own lantern on the ground and ran away when he was followed by a Lantern Man one night. 'When he ventured to look round there was the Lantern Man kicking the lantern over and over again.'

A Norfolk horseman also told Lady Cranworth of Letton some time before 1900, 'Folks du say that if one man stand at one end of the field and another man stand over agin him in the other corner, and they will whistle to each other, the Lantern Man will always run to the whistle.' He added, 'It is a good thing to know this as the Lantern Man will always try to come agin you and to kill ye, if so be he is able.'

Attacks by the Lantern Man were provoked by not treating him with respect. Mrs Lubbock recalled her father coming home with an old man who whistled and jeered at 'Jack', whereupon he followed them to the house and 'torched up at the windows'. About the same time, one evening in Horning, he knocked a man off his horse who mockingly called him 'Will o' the Wisp'.

Disbelief in him produced extreme reactions. Lady Cranworth relates a story told by an old Cromer fisherman, who said:

'There was a young fellow coming home one evening and he see the Lantern Man coming for him and he run; and that run! and he run again; and that run again! Now there was a silly old man . . . who didn't believe in none o' them things and this young fellow he run to his house and say, 'O Giles, for

Heaven's sake, let me in – the Lantern Man's coming!' And old Giles he say, 'You silly fool, there ain't no such thing as a Lantern Man.' But when he see the Lantern Man coming for him, Giles let the young fellow in . . . And old Giles, he thought he would play a trick on the Lantern Man so he got a candle and held that out of the window on the end of a pole. And . . . the Lantern Man he come for that and he burst it all to pieces.'

The Last Wolf

As late as 1806, an English school textbook said of the wolf:

. . . a savage aspect, a frightful howl, an insupportable odour, fierce habits, and a malignant disposition . . . render it dangerous and detested while living, and useless when dead.

Consequently, said the author, 'Hunting the wolf is . . . a species of the chase at which reason need not blush, nor humanity drop a tear.'

That wolves are bad is a time-honoured western tradition. To ancient Hindus and Zoroastrians, the wolf was evil and a symbol of evil in human nature; the Anglo-Saxon legal term *wulfesheofod* ('wolf-head') meant an outlaw with a price on his head; Vikings were 'wolves of the sea'; a sexual predator is still a 'wolf'.

Wolves traditionally preyed on human flesh – in Pictish, Anglo-Saxon, and Viking mythology and art they prowl battlefields, and in Guido, Bishop of Amiens's *Carmen de Bello Hastingensi* ('Song of the Battle of Hastings'), William the Conqueror leaves the bodies of the English to be devoured by worms, wolves, birds, and dogs.

The wolf was an arch-deceiver. Medieval bestiaries speak of the wolf spitting on its paws to make its approach inaudible or biting its paw if it stepped on a twig and alerted its prey (the wolf with a paw to its mouth appears in church carvings). In medieval tales, Isengrim the Wolf is as cunning as Reynard the Fox, often disguising himself, the proverbial 'wolf in sheep's clothing'.

'The Three Little Pigs', 'The Wolf and Seven Little Kids', 'Little Red Riding Hood' – from fairytales, too, people knew that wolves sneaked about in woods to deceive and devour children (or child-surrogates). In legends they heard of wolves snatching women and babies, as in the story of 'Wotobank', Beckermet, or the legend of Beth Gelert, Wales.

Wolves acting out of their traditional character were held up as marvels, from the she-wolf who suckled Romulus and Remus, to those in Scotland who likewise nurtured human babies, or so an old forester of the Reay said in the nineteenth century. The wolf-as-dog figures in saints' legends as evidence of their miraculous power, including the wolves who became civic guardians in the stories of St Francis and St Gens, and the wolf that guarded St Edmund's head near Hoxne, Suffolk.

Germanic peoples, admiring the wolf's ferocity, used 'wolf' in personal names, among them Old Norse Ulfr, 'wolf'; Old English Æthelwulf, 'wolf of royal lineage' and Cuthwulf, 'famous wolf'. It was an honourable name for the royal and military caste, but lesser ranks and women could bear it, so it often turns up in place-names derived from those of early landowners.

Other place-names testify to the presence of wolves in the past: Woolpit, Suffolk, OE *wulfpytt*, probably a pit to trap wolves; Wolford, Warwickshire, OE *wulf* + *weard*, 'guard', possibly an 'enclosure to protect flocks from wolves'; Wolborough, Devon, probably OE *wulfa-beorg*, 'wolves' hill', and Wolfhole Crag, Lancashire, probably OE *wulf-healh*, 'wolves' valley'.

Such names create a problem for 'last wolf' stories. That the last wolf in England was killed in Cheshire at the end of the fifteenth century *might* be true; or that it was slain at Humphrey Head. But it is unlikely to have been near the farmhouse named *Wolfa* near Great Salkeld in Cumberland, or at Wolverstone in Devon, any more than 'the last wolf in The Weald' is likely to have perished at 'Wolfscrag', West Chiltington, Sussex, despite three fields in the nineteenth century called Great Den, Little Den, and Far Den. These legends have almost certainly been inspired by the place-names.

With the wolf-slayer Jack of Badsaddle at Orlingbury, Northamptonshire, the hero-tale comes into play. Heroes need slayworthy opponents, and Jack is said to have killed a wolf or a boar or both.

'Last wolf' stories are normally connected with the landed gentry for historical reasons. Juliana Berners, in her *Book of St Albans*, *c.*1481, names the four beasts of venery as hart, hare, wolf, and boar. These were legitimate and respectable for noblemen to hunt on horseback. Richard Verstegan says that the Anglo-Saxons called January *wolf monath*, 'wolf month', because people were then 'in more danger to be devoured of Wolves than in any season else', and the medieval wolf-hunting season was 25 December to 25 March, though where they were an all-year-round menace open season was declared. Under the feudal system, tenants could hold land from overlords by the service of killing wolves – as late as the reign of Henry VI (1429–71), Sir Robert Plumpton held one bovate of land in Nottinghamshire called 'Wolf hunt land' by chasing wolves in Sherwood Forest.

Such service may have led to 'last wolf' stories. A family of the hereditary name of 'Wolfhunt' held lands at Wormhill, Derbyshire, in 1320, by wolf-hunting in the royal forest of the Peak, and a relative of the owner of Wormhill Hall remarked in *c.*1880, 'There is a tradition that the last Wolf in England was killed at Wormhill, but I never saw any evidence of it.'

Laying Ghosts

Traditionally, there are several ways to lay ghosts. Some require their bones to be found and buried; some are laid by prayer and Masses; others, who cannot rest because of some injustice done or suffered, vanish once this has been put right. Medieval Christians regarded them as souls undergoing punishment for sin, who could find peace through the prayers of the living. Occasionally, as in the twelfth-century accounts of William of Newburgh, revenants were malevolent undead corpses; these had to be physically destroyed.

Folk legends recorded in the nineteenth and twentieth centuries frequently describe a form of ghost laying which, paradoxically, is both religious and aggressive. These stories are set in the eighteenth or early nineteenth century; the ghosts are the stubborn, malevolent spectres of local evil-doers (often gentry) which disturb the whole community until a parson, or more often a group of parsons, confronts them and eventually subdues them by fierce and unceasing Bible-reading and prayer. The parsons usually hold lighted candles, which the ghost will try to extinguish; only men of the strongest faith can keep their candles burning and never falter in their prayers, a process which is often called 'reading down' the ghost. At Crackenthorpe and Lowther Castle, Westmorland, the exorcist is a Roman Catholic priest.

The purpose of this ritual is not to obtain entry into Heaven for the ghost, but to keep it bound to a specific spot on this earth; generally this is somewhere local, but sometimes it is the Red Sea. The ghost may be set an endless task, for example, making ropes of sand, emptying a lake with a small perforated shell, or stripping a hill of grass at the rate of one blade a night. Or it may be physically confined, often by being 'read down' into smaller and smaller forms and imprisoned in a bottle, snuff-box or boot, which is then thrown into a pool or river, or buried under a boulder. Sometimes, as at Okehampton, Devon, it is transformed into an animal, or forced to change from one animal shape to another less threatening one. In Cornwall, exorcizing parsons were said to use a whip to drive the ghost to some lonely spot where it would be confined to a small patch of ground.

A curious motif found in Devon and Somerset is that the ghost is returning steadily from its banishment, but only by the tiny distance of 'one cockstride' a year. Elsewhere, it may be said that it will return if the ivy reaches the top of some local building or bridge, or if the bottle in which it is imprisoned is broken, or the river into which it was thrown runs dry. Occasionally, the exorcist grants the ghost a limited period of freedom; at Little Lawford, Warwickshire, the ghost of One-Handed Boughton is allowed two hours' liberty every night.

A fine nineteenth-century tale of ceremonial ghost laying was set in the Gatley Carrs, a swampy area between Stockport, Northen (now Northenden), and

Didsbury (formerly Cheshire, now Greater Manchester). Fletcher Moss published it in 1884 'in the language of old folk who remember the occurrence'; they referred to the troublesome spirit as a 'boggart', which can mean either a troublesome goblin or a ghost. In the present case, the ghost was that of a miserly and dishonest grocer named Barrow, who had sold watered milk, and wailed horribly on moonlit nights.

Well, th'passon got everyone as 'ad a bible, an' them as could pray as well, an' when th'boggart was out at fu' moon they spread theirsels out, an' got round 'im, an' kept drawin' nigher an' nigher, an' th'boggart made back for th'churchyard, but they kep' 'im i' th'circle, an got 'im in a corner by th'yew tree, an' th'passon whips out a bit o' chalk an' draws a holy circle round th'place, an' aw th'folk join 'ands an' read their bibles, an' pray as 'ard as they could gabble, an' th'passon sings an' prays, an' bangs th'book, an 'ops about, an'poor ghost moans an' jabbers, an' chunners [mumbles], but they fair bet 'im an' smothert 'im wi' prayer, for th'devil was druv out o' 'im, an' now 'e lets 'im abide.

The combination of humour and drama is common in ghost-laying stories in nineteenth-century collections, and probably comes from the storytellers, not the collectors. Not only are they told in a racy style, but they can include details that are funny in themselves. At Pakenham, Suffolk, for example, the ghost is said to have been laid for a while inside a grandfather clock before being finally disposed of in a well.

Theo Brown, the only folklorist who has examined

stories of this type in any detail, believed that the idea of ghosts bound in confinement on this earth, or condemned to repetitive or impossible tasks, replaced belief in Purgatory, forbidden at the Reformation. But close comparison with traditions from Catholic countries would be required to test this interpretation.

The Mistletoe Bride

The story of the mistletoe bride was made the subject of a ballad by the songwriter Thomas Haynes Bayly (1797–1839), set to music by H. R. Bishop, and entitled 'The Mistletoe Bough' from its refrain, 'Oh! the Mistletoe Bough, Oh! the Mistletoe Bough.'

Its setting is the Christmas season, when 'the castle hall' is hung with mistletoe and holly. The company is 'blithe and gay', but the baron's beautiful daughter, 'young Lovel's bride', grows tired of dancing and starts to play hide-and-seek. Her friends and her lover search for her, but in vain: she cannot be found. The years roll by, until:

> At length an oak chest that had long lain hid,
> Was found in the castle. They raised the lid,
> And a skeleton form lay mouldering there,
> In the bridal wreath of the lady fair.

This song, also published in Bayly's *Songs, Ballads and Other Poems* (1844), was hugely popular at English village concerts in the Victorian and Edwardian eras. In the USA, too, it spread by word of mouth, sometimes being altered in the process – for example, the lost bride became a lost princess, or, as in an oral version collected in Kansas in 1959, the tune was scarcely changed but unfamiliar words had been replaced.

Because of the popularity of the song, several English 'halls' claimed to be the one in the story. A bride of the Lovel family of Skelton, Yorkshire, was generally held to be the original subject, and it was probably attracted to Minster Lovell, Oxfordshire, by the double coincidence of the same family name and the finding of a skeleton by workmen building a new chimney in 1708. The skeleton was that of a man, but the very word 'skeleton' seems to have been enough to hang the story on.

In Hampshire, it became attached to the Cope family of Bramshill House, where the Flower-de-Luce Room was said to be haunted by a ghost in bridal array, but was also said to have taken place at Marwell Old Hall and Malsanger. In Norfolk, it was set at Brockdish Hall near Harleston; in Somerset, depending on who you read, at either Bawdrip or Shapwick, where it is related to a stone in the church commemorating a local heiress who died on 14 June 1681, 'Taken away by a sudden and untimely fate at the very time of the marriage celebrations'.

The Minster Lovell, Bramshill, and Shapwick versions claim to be historical, but the evidence is tenuous. Marwell Old Hall could produce the very chest in which the bride died, but so could Bramshill. Joan Penelope Cope, as a child of twelve, wrote:

The chest was in the possession of our family . . . until about a hundred and twenty years ago the tenth baronet, Sir Denzil's widow took it away to her people. My great-grandfather wrote to the present owner saying; 'if your heart is in the right place, you will send back my chest.' . . . But he only wrote back: '. . . My heart is in the right place . . . it is in my chest,' and so he kept it.

The Marwell Old Hall chest was allegedly preserved into the twentieth century at nearby Upham Rectory. But most old houses possessed chests, once a stock piece of storage, and some may have been bridal chests, holding the bride's clothes and household linen and going with her to her new home. These carried her initials and the date of her wedding, and may have provided the link with the notion of a bride. The rest followed. As Robert Chambers remarks, 'The chest is big enough to be a tomb for a human being: therefore it was so.'

There appears to be no European version of the legend, suggesting that it arose in England. Though conceivably based on a historical incident, surviving versions are undoubtedly the same story, with only minor variations. It was probably current by the eighteenth century, as it forms the plot of 'Ginevra' in Samuel Rogers's blank verse poem *Italy* (1822–8). Only in this and one other instance did he take his themes from neither Italian history nor tradition. He observes, 'This story is, I believe, founded on fact; although the time and place are uncertain. Many old houses in England lay claim to it.'

His version is set in Modena, in an old palace of the Orsini. There, in an empty room, stands an oak chest, on the wall above it a portrait of a beautiful girl named Ginevra. The last of her race, at fifteen she married 'her first love', Francesco Doria. Ginevra enjoyed the irrepressible high spirits of youth and was given to 'pranks'. The day of the wedding arrived, but she failed to appear at the bridal feast and could not be found. Heartbroken, Francesco threw his life away fighting the Turk; Ginevra's father, old Orsini, died; and the house went to strangers.

> Full fifty years were past, and all forgot,
> When on an idle day, a day of search
> Mid the old lumber in the Gallery,
> That mouldering chest was noticed . . .

They try to move it:

> but on the way
> It burst, it fell; and lo, a skeleton,
> With here and there a pearl, an emerald-stone,
> A golden clasp, clasping a shred of gold.
> All else had perished – save a nuptial ring,
> And a small seal, her mother's legacy,
> Engraven with a name, the name of both,
>   'Ginevra.'

Mother Shipton

In 1641 appeared a pamphlet, *The Prophesie of Mother Shipton*. This claims that Mother Shipton lived in Tudor times and foretold the downfall of Cardinal Wolsey; it also asserts that she had been born in a cave near the Dropping Well at Knaresborough, Yorkshire, in 1488, had married a certain Toby Shipton in 1512, and died in her seventies. However, despite these realistic details, there is no trace of her in parish records, which makes it unlikely that she ever existed. Seventeenth-century pamphleteers often inserted plausible but fictitious details. A later pamphlet, Richard Head's *The Life and Death of Mother Shipton* (1667) is frankly fabulous, as is the anonymous *Strange and Wonderful History of Mother Shipton* (1686). Head says she was the child of the Devil and a nun (like Merlin), played magical tricks on people, and rode about in a chariot drawn by stags, accompanied by her imps. Illustrations usually show her as a hump-backed, hook-nosed crone, often wearing the typical pointed witch's hat.

Her clash with Cardinal Wolsey is a consistent feature of the early pamphlets. Hearing he intended to visit York, she remarked that although he might *see* it, he would never enter it. Not long afterwards, Wolsey, on his way to York, halted for the night some eight miles (13 km) away; that very night he was arrested, without ever setting foot in the city. Political prophecies attributed to Mother Shipton were exploited in the Civil War, and linked to other major events. In his *Diary* for 20 October 1666, Pepys, discussing the Great Fire of London, writes that Prince Rupert had commented that 'now Shipton's prophecy was out', i.e. its true meaning revealed. There is nothing relevant to the Fire among the sayings now preserved, but others probably circulated at the time.

Nowadays, Shipton's fame rests on the claim that she foretold various modern inventions and phenomena. Most of these supposed prophecies were deliberate fabrications. In Brighton in 1862, Charles Hindley, a hack writer and publisher, produced *The Life, Prophecies and Death of the Famous Mother Shipton*. He claims it is a verbatim reprint of a pamphlet of 1684, as indeed the early sections are; however, there are also twenty-two rhyming prophecies that are simply Hindley's own invention. They contain clear allusions to such Victorian discoveries and events as steam power, telegraphy, railways, ballooning, the Crystal Palace, the Crimean War, and the Gold Rush (modern interpreters, however, claim the 'horseless carriages' as cars, not trains), and hint at cosmic upheavals:

> Water shall yet more wonders do
> Now, strange shall yet be true,
> The world upside down shall be,
> And gold found at the root of tree.

Finally, the date of Doomsday was dramatically revealed:

> The world then to an end shall come
> In eighteen hundred and eighty-one.

This date remains the same when read forwards, backwards, or upside down, which probably seemed ominous.

In 1872, a correspondent to *Notes and Queries* inquired about these verses; a few months later the editor reported that Hindley had admitted inventing them. But the faked prophecy persisted. The verses were often reprinted, with slight variations, but always saying the world would end in 1881. When the fatal year arrived, panic ensued, especially around Brighton, where many people spent the nights praying in the open fields. One death was directly attributable to the panic: the inquest on a ten-year-old London girl called Kate Weedon was told how 'she frequently cried and talked about the world coming to an end' that year, and on 17 November became hysterical, 'saying she knew the end of the world would come in the night'. She went into a violent fit, and died before morning.

Mother Shipton's prophecies are still sold at Knaresborough, and can be found on the Internet; during most of the twentieth century, Doomsday was announced for 1991 – a date which can at least be read back to front, though not upside down. Currently, no exact date is mentioned; instead, 'the world shall end when High Bridge is thrice fallen', this being a Knaresborough bridge which has already collapsed twice.

The Mowing Devil

In 1678, a pamphlet was published entitled:

The Mowing-Devil: Or, Strange *NEWS* out of Hartford-shire. Being a True Relation of a Farmer, who Bargaining with a poor *Mower*, about the Cutting down Three Half Acres of *Oats*; upon the *Mower*'s asking too much, the *Farmer* swore *That the Devil should Mow it rather than He*. And so it fell out, that very Night, the Crop of *Oat* shew'd as if it had been all of a Flame; but next Morning appear'd so neatly Mow'd by the Devil, or some Infernal Spirit, that no Mortal Man was able to do the like . . .

Though presented as 'News', the story is admonitory, a punishment for blasphemy, it being well known that 'naming the Devil summons him'.

The title page bears a woodcut showing a black-horned figure at work with his scythe amid concentric circles of grain. This has often been noted by cerealogists (students of crop circles), though modern computer-designed circles are infinitely more elaborate. Whereas now they are often said to be produced by extra-terrestrials, they were formerly attributed to the Devil.

The idea of the Devil as a mower appears in a wide-spread tale, 'The mowing contest', in Norfolk attached to Sir Barney Brograve of Worstead and Waxham Hall;

in Kentchurch, Herefordshire, to the wizard Jack o' Kent; and in Northamptonshire to a farmer who outwits 'Bogey' (the Devil).

More important is the international theme of 'Demon travels in whirlwind', the Devil or other evil spirit often carrying off some adept in magic, from an Arctic shamaness to the witch of Fraddam, Cornwall, whom the enchanter of Pengersick Castle whisked off through the air. At Leverington in Cambridgeshire, the annual feast used to take place on 'Whirlin' Sunday', and *Fenland Notes and Queries* (1891) reports that 'Whirlwind cakes' made for the occasion were explained by the story that an old lady making cakes for the feast was carried off by the Devil in a whirlwind, according to later versions as a punishment for baking on Sunday.

Behind these stories lie early interpretations of 'dust devils' or 'land devils'. Unless they cause substantial damage, tornados and whirlwinds in England often go unreported: only one of seven recorded on 1 December 1975 was mentioned in the press. Yet a list of tornados occurring between 1951 and 1991, compiled by Mike Rowe of the Tornado and Storm Research Organisation, included three 'land-devils', a waterspout, and twenty tornados, one of them violent, in Norfolk alone.

This sheds light on the mysterious 'Roger's Blast', defined by the Revd Robert Forby in 1830 as 'a sudden and local motion of the air . . . whirling up the dust on a dry road in perfectly calm weather, somewhat in the manner of a water-spout'. These rotatory winds, which lay corn and reeds in a circle, in East Anglia are sometimes violent: reports speak of windmills wrecked, yachts and wherries grounded, trees felled, roofs torn off, windows smashed. A 'wind-rush' in Essex in 1916 lifted a boy off his bike and onto a hedge, while an oral account of a 'roger' (as they are now known), in the 1930s, says it lifted a shed and whirled it away, leaving bricklayers inside it unharmed.

In 1866, a fairly fruitless discussion opened up in regional journals and newspapers as to who 'Roger' might be, suggestions including the medieval scholar and reputed Master Magician Roger Bacon; the supposedly bad-tempered Roger Bigod of Bungay Castle; Sir Roger L'Estrange (1616–1704); and Sir Roger Ascham (1515–68). The most useful suggestion came from someone who noted the word *Rowdyonys* in the medieval *Promptorium Parvulorum*, and philologists today derive 'Roger's Blast' from Middle English *rodion*, a whirlwind, also *rodiones blaste* or *rowdynys blaste*, described in 1430–40 as 'A whirle wynd blowing nothing softe . . . That reiseth duste & strauh ful hih alofte.'

Like 'Old Nick' and 'Old Harry', 'Old Roger' moreover appears as a name for the Devil from 1725. People have long attributed tempests and other meteorological phenomena to the wrath of God, often working through the Devil – compare the Black Dog of Bungay, Suffolk. The connection between the Devil, storms, and destruction of crops is also expressed in the tradition of 'sky-ships'. Gervase of Tilbury (*c.* 1150–*c.*1220) writes that, in 1211, people coming out of church on a dark cloudy day saw a ship's cable stretching down from above the clouds. Though a sailor tried to climb down it, he perished in our air. As Agobard, Archbishop of Lyons in the ninth century, explained:

We have seen and heard many who . . . assert that there is a . . . country which they call *Magonia*, whence ships come in the clouds for the purpose of carrying back the corn which is beaten off by the hail and storms; and which these aërial sailors purchase of the *tempestarii* [storm-fiends].

The ship's cable reaching into the clouds is an apt metaphor for a small tornado, and from sky-ships it is a short step to UFOs.

Mr Fox

The same story may be told in different ways, to serve different purposes. 'The Glass Ball', collected by S. O. Addy at Norton, is a fairytale version of one told elsewhere as a legend – the tale of a false lover who murders or attempts to murder a girl; it is often localized, told as true, and involves an open grave (though in one version this is seen in a dream). These stories include 'The Oxford Student'; 'The Lonton Lass', from Yorkshire; 'The Girl who Got up the Tree', from North Derbyshire; 'The Lass 'at Seed her Awn Graave Dug', from Lindsey, Lincolnshire; and a song from Somerset aptly entitled 'False Foxes'. In the story of 'Bloody Baker' told at Cranbrook, Kent, the story has become attached to a historical person, Sir Richard Baker, builder of Sissinghurst Castle.

In the Lindsey story, the villain is called Mr Fox, and in 'The Glass Ball' said to be one. In 'Mr Fox's Courtship' from Somerset, though not named in the story itself, he is described as a 'red-headed hosebud', or rascal. Implicit is the traditional description of foxes as 'red', and a range of metaphorical expressions, 'sly as a fox' and 'foxy' in the sense of 'crafty'. The fox is also elegant – a good symbol for a handsome seducer.

Whether they mention foxes or not, all these stories relate, some more closely than others, to another fairytale, 'Mr Fox'. This tells of the beautiful Lady Mary, who has met a Mr Fox at her father's country mansion. 'No one knew who Mr Fox was; but he was certainly brave, and surely rich.' She agrees to marry him, but though Mr Fox describes his castle, he does not invite her there.

Just before the wedding, Lady Mary sets out for the castle when Mr Fox is supposedly away. What happens next is first told by the narrator, then recapitulated by Lady Mary in a denouement which is a storytelling triumph. At a wedding breakfast before they sign the contract, Mr Fox says she seems pale. She replies she has had bad dreams:

'I dreamed,' said Lady Mary, 'that I went yestermorn to your castle, and I found it in the woods . . . and over the gateway was written:

Be bold, be bold.'

'But it is not so, nor it was not so,' said Mr Fox.

'And when I came to the doorway, over it was written:

Be bold, be bold, but not too bold.'

'It is not so, nor it was not so,' said Mr Fox.

'And then I went upstairs, and came to . . . a door, on which was written:

Be bold, be bold, but not too bold,
Lest that your heart's blood should run cold.'

'It is not so, nor it was not so,' said Mr Fox.

'And then . . . I opened the door, and the room was filled with bodies and skeletons of poor dead women, all stained with their blood.'

'It is not so, nor it was not so. And God forbid it should be so,' said Mr Fox.

She then tells him she dreamt that, as she was fleeing down the stairs, she saw him dragging behind him a rich and beautiful young woman. He denies it in the same words. She replies that she just had time to hide before he passed her, and she saw him hack the young woman's hand off with his sword to get her diamond ring. Again he denies it with his customary refrain. Then Lady Mary cries, 'But it is so, and it was so. Here's hand and ring I have to show', and she pulls out the lady's hand from her dress. 'At once her brothers and her friends drew their swords and cut Mr Fox into . . . pieces.'

'Mr Fox' may be a very old fairytale, already current around 1600 when Shakespeare wrote *Much Ado About Nothing*. Mr Fox's refrain echoes one referred to by Benedick in Act 1, scene 1: 'Like the old tale, my lord, "It is not so, nor t'was not so, but indeed, God forbid it should be so."' 'Mr Fox' itself was contributed to Edmond Malone's *Variorum Shakespeare* (1790) in illustration of this. It had been learned from an old lady born in 1715.

'Mr Fox' combines themes also found in 'The Robber Bridegroom' in the Grimms' *Kinder- und Hausmärchen* (1812–15), with the motif of the 'forbidden chamber' found in Charles Perrault's fairytale 'Bluebeard'. The basic plot of all versions concerns a girl who has exposed herself to danger from a man of whom she knows little, whether she does this through some moral fault (sex before marriage, social climbing, greed); through taking no notice of warnings and warning signs (such as Bluebeard's unnatural beard); or through simple curiosity.

When told as a local legend, it is very much a story for adults; it has a happier counterpart among nursery tales for children. The fox was proverbial for both wiliness and rapacity, and for having no mercy on hens. 'The Fox and the Little Red Hen' concerns a little red hen who lives on the edge of a wood. On the far side of the wood lives a robber fox. He catches the Little Red Hen and takes her home to his mother to cook. Again it is the tale of a male predator who is an outsider and his female prey. But the Little Red Hen, like Lady Mary, escapes her fate by her own cunning, which surpasses that of the fox.

Robin Hood

The Robin Hood story is unusually plausible. The hero and his companions are outlaws living by robbery and poaching, outwitting the forces of law (commonly, the sheriff of Nottingham). Eventually Robin encounters 'King Edward', who, impressed by Robin's courtesy, pardons him and calls him to live at court. This finale is admittedly unconvincing, and so are some elements added in later literary sources – Robin as a dispossessed earl, Maid Marian, King John's villainy – but the basic story is realistic. Could Robin have been real?

Three identifications have been suggested: Robert Hod, who fled from York in 1226 because he owed money to a church there; a valet named Robyn Hode who was a servant of Edward II at York in 1324, but then left his service; and a Robin Hood who trespassed in a royal forest at Rockingham, Northamptonshire, in 1354. But 'Robin' and 'Hood' are both common names. The basic sources disagree on the setting for the outlaw's activities. Andrew of Wyntoun, the first chronicler to mention him (c.1420), places him first in Inglewood, near Carlisle, and then in Barnsdale, near York. Some ballads mention Barnsdale, others Sherwood Forest and Nottingham. There being three medieval King Edwards, the dating is also wide open, especially since an alternative tradition (beginning c.1500) puts Robin in the reign of Richard I (1189–99).

The legend was never shaped into a single inclusive narrative, but its popularity is obvious from many passing allusions. Games, pageants, and brief plays featuring Robin were a regular form of entertainment, especially at church festivals on May Day and Midsummer. He appears in thirty-nine ballads from the late fifteenth century to the eighteenth, and four brief scripts for Elizabethan playlets. These primary sources circle repeatedly round a few basic themes. Robin is an outlaw, though no ballad explains why. He has companions, the most important being Little John, who is almost his equal in skill and strength. Physical prowess is stressed in the many archery competitions and bouts of wrestling or quarterstaff fighting; cunning and trickery are valued too: many stories involve disguise and plots.

Robin's death through treachery is mentioned in only three early texts – two ballads, and Richard Grafton's unsympathetic *Chronicle* of 1569:

For the sayd Robert Hood, being afterwardes troubled with sicknesse, came to a certain Nonry in Yorkshire called Bircklies [Kirklees], wher desiring to be let blood, he was betrayed and bled to death. After whose death the Prioresse of the same place caused him to be buried by the highway side, where he had vsed to rob and spoyle those that passed that way . . . And the cause why she buryed him there, was for that the common passengers and travailers knowing and seeing him there buryed, might more safely and without feare take their iorneys that way, which they durst not do in the life of the sayd outlawes. And at either end of the sayde Tombe was erected a crosse of stone, which is to be seene there at this present.

According to the two early ballads, the prioress was Robin's kinswoman, and her lover, a knight, stabbed him while he was weakened by the blood-letting. A much later one, from the eighteenth century, adds that he shot one last arrow through the window, asking to be buried where it fell.

Nowadays, the essential element in Robin's character is that he 'robbed the rich to give to the poor', so it is a shock to find that in early texts Robin almost always keeps his winnings for himself and his men; in one ballad, however, he does give part to an impoverished knight. That ballad ends:

> For he was a good outlaw,
> And did poor men much good.

From the 1580s on, the story is elaborated and transformed. In a play by Anthony Munday (1601), Robin is rightful Earl of Huntingdon in Richard I's reign, outlawed through his wicked uncle's plot, and his fiancée is wooed by Prince John (though the latter is not yet a villain). Sir Walter Scott, in *Ivanhoe*, gives the tradition a political twist: his Robin supports the Saxon Ivanhoe against wicked Norman barons; this theme too was frequently copied by others. By the end of the nineteenth century, Robin typefied light-hearted courage, cheeky defiance of tyranny, healthy country living, generosity, comradeship, and patriotism. His popularity continues through cinema and television.

Secret Passages

One of the most frequent ideas among local tales and traditions is that there are secret tunnels linking certain buildings, usually those that are old and well known in the district. Many instances have been mentioned in folklore collections and regional books, usually associated with castles, churches, large isolated houses, and old inns. Most are said to run from one building to another, but some are believed to go down to the sea, or to a river, or occasionally into the depths of a hill. Those who talk or write about them usually believe that they exist, or did in the past, and can sometimes point to short lengths of tunnelling that have been found in the vicinity of some old building as evidence; unfortunately, these have generally turned out, on investigation, to be the remains of drains, water conduits, wine vaults, or ice houses. In contrast, the tunnels of rumour and tradition are by no means short; they are often described as running for miles, and sometimes through very unsuitable terrain where any such structure would soon collapse or become blocked – passing under riverbeds, for instance, or through swampy ground. Stories making claims on this scale must be regarded as legendary, not factual, however firmly the beliefs may be held.

The bare statement that a tunnel exists is often embellished by an explanation of why it was built, by reference to the history – real or imagined – of the building(s) it is linked to. At Rottingdean, Sussex, the many old houses in the centre of the village are all said to be linked to one another by a network of underground passages used by smugglers, which fits well with known history. At Beeston Castle, Cheshire, and at many other castles which are known to have been besieged, the tunnel is alleged to have been dug out to enable the defenders to escape; similarly, monks at Whitby Abbey, Yorkshire, are said to have had one leading to Robin Hood's Bay, more than a mile (1.6 km) away, for safety in time of war. Old houses that once belonged to Catholic gentry are often reputed to have tunnels enabling priests to escape in times of persecution. As a result of Protestant propaganda alleging that sexual misconduct was widespread in religious communities, many ruined abbeys and priories are said to have tunnels leading to a nunnery some miles off, to facilitate amorous trysts.

Tales of treasure are readily associated with tunnels. Some stories mention a supernatural creature lurking there to prevent access; the nineteenth-century Sussex folklore collector Charlotte Latham was informed that a two-mile (3-km) tunnel leading from Offington to the hill-fort of Cissbury Ring contained a pot of gold guarded by two immense serpents. Or the storytellers may draw upon history, as when the Cheshire writer J. H. Ingram was told in the 1940s that after Birkenhead priory was closed down at the Reformation several monks fled down an underground passage with the prior's gold, but the roof caved in and neither monks nor gold were ever seen again. Interest in such matters can still be strong.

In December 2004 and January 2005 there were press articles about a network of tunnels allegedly running beneath the streets of Hertford, hiding 'treasures of immense importance' that perhaps included the Holy Grail. This was based on the historical fact that four Knights Templar were imprisoned in Hertford Castle in 1309 on the orders of Edward II, who wanted to confiscate their wealth; the reports have been much publicized by members of a modern Templar Order based in the town.

Traditional narratives involving tunnels hold out little hope that anyone will succeed in finding a crock of gold and bringing it safely back. On the contrary, they stress that exploring underground carries risks that can easily prove fatal. Writing in 1974, Jeremy Errand reported 'a choice myth' from Arundel, Sussex, namely that a man entered an underground passage leading from the castle, accompanied by his dog, but neither was ever seen again; a variant version claims it was a duck, not a dog, and that the bird 'emerged from the ground about five miles away a fortnight after the man's disappearance'. (The river valley below the castle is often flooded, which may be why a duck was thought more likely to survive the experience.)

The most dramatic type of tunnel narrative is that of the lost musician, told of some half-dozen places in England and often linked to the place-name Fiddler's Copse. This tells how some men want to test the truth of a tradition that places A and B, two or three miles (3–5 km) apart, are linked by a tunnel, the entrance to which can be seen at A. They decide that one of them, a fiddler, will go down at A and walk along the passage, playing a tune as he goes; his companions track him at ground level by following the music. All goes well at first, but about halfway along the expected route the music stops, abruptly and completely. The fiddler never reappears, and nobody dares go down to find out what has happened. Instead, his companions plant Fiddler's Copse above the spot where his fate overtook him.

The Seven Whistlers

On 24 March 1855, this appeared in the *Leicester Chronicle*:

On Friday, the 16th inst., a collier . . . was asked by a tradesman . . . why he was not at his usual work. The reply . . . was that none of the men had gone to work . . . because they had heard the 'Seven Whistlers,' . . . birds sent by Providence to warn them of an impending danger, and . . . when they heard that signal not a man would go down the pit . . .

When the tradesman suggested this was just superstition, the collier was offended and told him that, twice before, the Seven Whistlers were heard but colliers still went down the pit, and two lives were lost on each occasion.

The same belief was held in Warwickshire. *The Times* for 21 September 1874 reported that men working at Bedworth Collieries refused to go down the coal-pits one Monday as during Sunday night the Seven Whistlers had been heard in the neighbourhood.

Whereas Arthur Evans, in *Leicestershire Words* (1881), classes the Seven Whistlers as 'superstition', the tradition treads the fine line between supernatural belief and legend, for people had their own ideas about the identity of the supernatural visitants and could tell apparently true stories in vindication of their belief.

Evans says, 'what the Seven Whistlers may be I

never could learn'. However, the *Leicester Chronicle* on 12 February 1853 had printed an origin legend told by the colliers themselves. According to this, seven colliers got drunk one Sunday, and towards nightfall decided to whistle as a wager to pay for more drink. They were instantly whisked up into the clouds by a whirlwind. Each night, as darkness falls, they 'fly from place to place, when fatal accidents are impending, to warn . . . their survivors to avoid their own terrific and never-dying destiny'.

Men in another dangerous calling also believed in the Whistlers, as Francis Buckland learned from one of the oldest fishermen in Folkestone in the mid nineteenth century:

'I never thinks any good of them,' said old Smith; 'there's always an accident when they comes. I heard 'em once one dark night last winter. They come over our heads all of a sudden, singing 'ewe-ewe,' and the men in the boat wanted to go back. It came on to rain and blow soon afterwards . . . and, sure enough, before morning, a boat was upset, and seven poor fellows drowned.

Old Smith was under no illusions about what he had actually heard. 'I know what makes the noise, sir; it's them long-bill'd curlews; but I never likes to hear them.'

The Seven Whistlers were identified with several species of bird, including swifts in Leicestershire, teal and widgeon in Derbyshire, and golden plovers. But knowing that birds made the noise is not the same thing as ascribing their advent to natural causes. Belief was once widespread in direct intervention by God in human affairs, often through the agency of birds, and also in the existence of 'soul-birds', thought to house the souls of the drowned. Some said that the Seven Whistlers, too, were the spirits of comrades returning to warn their fellows.

The *Leicester Chronicle* describes the sound of the Whistlers as at times 'resembling the smothered wailings of children'. Behind this may lie a tradition like that in Portugal, where the whistles were attributed to widgeon believed to embody the souls of unbaptized children. In the north of England, The Gabriel Hounds, sometimes identified with the Whistlers, were also connected with unchristened infants, the implication being that they are doomed to wander because they could not enter Heaven.

William Wordsworth calls the Seven Whistlers 'the seven birds . . . that never part', but Worcestershire people believed that six of them flew about continually looking for the seventh. Jabez Allies, in the forepart of the nineteenth century, recorded what would happen when they found him:

. . . I have been informed by Mr J. Pressdee . . . that, when a boy, he frequently heard his late grandfather . . . who lived . . . in Suckley, say that oftentimes, at night . . . he heard six out of the 'Seven Whistlers' pass over his head, but that no more than six of them were ever heard . . . and that should the seven whistle together the world would be at an end.

The Leicestershire belief that the Whistlers were doomed to a 'never-dying destiny' was shared by Lanca-

shire, though differently explained. A contributor to
Notes and Queries in 1871 reported that an old man, on
hearing the whistling overhead of plovers, remarked
that, when he was a boy, the old people considered it a
bad omen to hear 'the wandering Jews' and explained,
'There is a tradition that they contain the souls of . . .
Jews who assisted at the crucifixion, and . . . are doomed
to float in the air for ever.'

This places the Seven Whistlers in their rightful context: they belong with the wild aerial hunts led by
undying kings – Charlemagne, Waldemar, Arthur – and
with those grand legendary sinners doomed to death-in-
life, the Wandering Jew and the Flying Dutchman.

Shakespeare in Legend

The most famous author in the English language inspired a number of legends and traditions in Warwickshire, his native county. Besides 'Shakespeare's chair', long preserved at Stratford-on-Avon, 'Shakespeare's bench' from a local pub, along with his half-pint mug, were said in 1794 to be well known to English antiquaries.

When the Hon. John Byng visited Stratford in 1781, he made a beeline for the church to see Shakespeare's tomb and noted 'some good old monuments of the Clopton family . . . in whose park did this Mr Shakespear divert himself by stealing venison'. He then mentions another poaching tradition, current within a hundred years of Shakespeare's death, attached to Charlcote Park.

Charlcote had been home to the Lucy family since 1247, and its owner in Shakespeare's time was Sir Thomas Lucy. Supposedly, on being prosecuted by Sir Thomas for stealing deer more than once from Charlcote Park, Shakespeare out of revenge wrote a ballad against him. This was so bitter that it redoubled Sir Thomas's fury and Shakespeare was forced to leave Stratford for London. Some add that, had it not been for this exile, Shakespeare might never have written his plays.

Shakespeare's ballad was said by the first recorder of the poaching tradition, Nicholas Rowe, in his edition of

Shakespeare (1709–10), to have been lost. However, Byng quotes from an old manuscript in his possession these words, allegedly sung for many years at Stratford:

> Sir Thomas was too covetous
> To covet so much deer;
> When horns enough upon his head
> Most plainly did appear.
>
> Had not his worship one deer left,
> What then he had a wife
> Took pains enough to find him horns
> Shou'd hold him during life.

Byng says that Joshua Barnes, Professor of Greek at Cambridge, heard an old woman at a Stratford inn singing the ballad in about 1690, and gave her a new gown for these two verses, 'and could she have said it all, he would . . . have given her ten guineas'.

The antiquary William Oldys (1696–1761) preserved the tradition that Shakespeare's 'bitter ballad' was nailed to the gate at Charlcote Park, and quotes all that could be remembered by Thomas Jones of Turbich, Worcestershire, who died in 1703, aged upwards of ninety. Jones said he had often heard the story from old people in Stratford:

> A parliemente member, a justice of peace,
> At home a poor scare-crowe, at London an asse,
> If lowsie is Lucy, as some volke miscalle it,
> Then Lucy is lowsie whatever befall it:

> He thinks himself great,
> Yet an asse in his state
> We allowe by his ears but with asses to mate.
> If Lucy is lowsie, as some volke miscalle it,
> Sing lowsie Lucy, whatever befall it.

Self-evidently a different ballad, this is thought to be from Charles II's time.

As to historical basis, Mrs Lucy of Charlcote told William Howitt, author of *Visits to Remarkable Places* (1840), that it was untrue that Shakespeare was caught poaching at Charlcote – it was in the old park at Fulbrook. Howitt gleaned this, while walking in Charlcote Park, from a country lad, who pointed out a statue as being 'Shakespeare on a deer'. On closer inspection, Howitt realized it was actually 'Diana with a Stag'. This lead statue, shown on a map of 1791 at the end of the lime avenue, disappeared early in the nineteenth century.

Then there was 'Shakespeare's Crab-Tree', by the roadside near Bidford on the way to Stratford. Shakespeare was supposedly a convivial fellow, who played shovelboard at the Falcon in Stratford, and danced on a particular flagstone in the floor of the Shoulder of Mutton at Broad Marston. The *Gentleman's Magazine* in 1794 tells the story of two bands of drinking cronies, the Topers and the Sippers. The Topers challenged all comers, and Shakespeare with other lads from Stratford took them on. They were to meet on Whit Sunday at Bidford, but when they arrived found only the Sippers, the Topers having gone to another match. To their mortification, the heads of even the Sippers proved to be stronger than theirs, so, conceding victory while still having the use of their legs, they set off home:

On the way, they lay down to sleep it off under a wide-spreading crab-tree. Next morning, when they woke and someone suggested they go back to Bidford to start over, Shakespeare refused, exclaiming, 'Farewell':

> 'Piping Pebworth, dancing Marston,
> Haunted Hillbro', hungry Grafton,
> Dodging Exhall, Popish Wicksford,
> Beggarly Brome, and drunken Bidford!'

Although the story of 'Shakespeare's Crab-Tree' was long known in Warwickshire, it is probably apocryphal, built around pre-existing nicknames. However, it added a landmark to 'Shakespeare country' until the tree died and in 1824 was felled.

Shuck

The Revd E. S. Taylor of Ormesby wrote in 1850 that he had heard of Shuck from many people in East Norfolk and Cambridgeshire, who described him as a 'black shaggy dog, with fiery eyes . . . who visits churchyards at midnight'.

He had particular 'beats': the Quaker writer Amelia Opie, when staying at Northrepps Cottage in January 1829 and after walking by Overstrand church, wrote in her journal, 'Tradition says, that every evening, at twilight, the *ghost of a dog* is seen to pass under the wall of this churchyard, having begun its walk from the church at B– [Beeston] . . . It is known by the name of Old Shuck.' His route ran towards the present Cromer railway station, thence along the coast. In the 1920s, though it had been built over, locals still knew it as 'Shuck's Lane'.

The Revd John Gunn, rector of Irstead, in 1849 reported an elderly parishioner as saying that Shuck ran nightly over Coltishall Bridge. She also told of a local encounter:

Finch, of Neatishead, was walking in the road after dark, and saw a dog . . . he thought was Dick Allard's, that had snapped and snarled at him . . . Along came the dog, straight in the middle of the road, and Finch kicked at him; and his foot went through him, as through . . . paper . . .

Shuck has now become a hallmark of East Anglian folklore, and reduced to a stereotype. In books and newspapers, he is almost invariably described as a black dog who is ominous to meet. This ignores the variety of both printed texts and oral testimony.

Shuck is not a true Black Dog but one of many shape-shifting Bogey Beasts. Local manifestations include 'Old Scarf', haunting Southtown Road, Great Yarmouth, and 'Skeff' of Garvestone; 'Old Shocks', who in 1894 was to be seen in the lane leading from Tasburgh to Flordon railway station; the 'Shucky Dog' around Magdalen, in about 1900; and 'Chuff', recorded in Walberswick, Suffolk, in the 1980s. Similar to Old Scarf was 'Owd Rugman', a spectral dog who haunted the neighbourhood of Lenwade and Lyng (a kind of dog called a 'water-rug' is mentioned by Shakespeare).

In 1830, 'Old Shock' was said to appear in the form of a dog *or* a calf; in Suffolk 'Shock' sometimes had a donkey's head, and around Geldeston the 'Hateful Thing', though seeming at times a black dog, might be identical with a spectral donkey haunting the same ground. Old Scarf might appear as a black goat; the Faines of Hethersett were 'the size of calves'; while West Wratting, Cambridgeshire, boasted a Shug Monkey.

Collectors hearing of headless dogs with saucer eyes made jokes about it. However, headlessness and saucer eyes are traditional signs of the supernatural. These eyes, which distinguished Old Scarf, Skeff of Garvestone, and the Hethersett Faines, and 'the eyes . . . like railway lamps' reported by a man who encountered Shuck in the 1930s near St Olave's, are the great round eyes of the dogs in Hans Andersen's *Tinder Box*.

An old keeper told Emily, Lady Cranworth of Letton, *c.*1900, that Skeff's coat was 'all skeffy-like . . . like an old sheep', while Mrs Opie in 1829 said a gamekeeper who felt Old Shock's coat one night described it as 'rough, hard, and shaggy'. This accords with his name. Though formally derived from Old English *scucca*, meaning 'devil, fiend', *shucky* is also Norfolk dialect for 'shaggy' – hence Magdalen's Shucky Dogs. Shuck's coat relates him to 'Mounsieur Shagg', the supernatural Black Dog of Newgate, London, described in 1638 as appearing before executions. The 'shoughs' mentioned in Shakespeare's *Macbeth* are explained by Dr Johnson as 'what we now call shocks'.

The shock or shock-dog was a dog with shaggy hair, especially a poodle, and if today this seems inappropriate to our idea of phantom Black Dogs, according to Patricia Dale Green in *Dog* (1966), 'in northern Europe at least a sixth of all dog-demons are black poodles.' Given that Shuck in some manifestations was white, perhaps into this background fits Boy, the white standard poodle accused of being Prince Rupert's familiar and killed at Marston Moor.

A hint of Shuck's demonic ancestry comes from *Seinte Marharete* (St Margaret), written in the late twelfth or early thirteenth century. It features an 'invisible un-wight', who also appears in animal form, calls himself a 'bitter beast' and creeps on his belly like a dog when reprimanded. Marharete calls him *alde schuke*, 'old shock'.

Though, according to Walter Rye, to meet Shuck means death within the year, this is not borne out in oral tradition. Shuck and the Black Dog of Bungay, Suffolk, have to some extent merged since the late nineteenth century, and out of seventy-four 'sightings' compiled in 1977, only seventeen could be connected with death or misfortune.

Just as in Lincolnshire Black Dogs escorted women down lonely lanes at night, so Shuck may act as a guardian. A man from Bawburgh was reported in 1988 as saying that, one night, he had to get out of the road because a huge hound with eyes 'like coals of fire' stood in his way. This prevented his being run down by a car with no lights. 'All I can say is, on that night he saved my life.'

Skulls

Collectors of ghost lore have often noted that a number of old houses contain, or formerly contained, a human skull regarded as a protective, luck-bringing talisman. Its presence is no secret; on the contrary, it is a source of pride to the owners of the house (generally a long-established family), and is kept in some particular resting place, often one where it can be plainly viewed. The recent study by Andy Roberts and David Clarke identifies twenty-seven examples. In every case, there is a strong tradition that the skull must never be removed; this is generally backed by anecdotes claiming that some attempt was once made to get rid of it, by burying it or throwing it into a pond, but there followed such troublesome ghostly commotion that nobody could sleep, as at Chilton Cantelo, Somerset. Sometimes there were worse disasters too – disease among cattle, outbreaks of fire, even deaths. Peace would always be restored when the skull was brought back, or when it inexplicably reappeared of its own accord. In every case, there is also some story to explain whose skull it is and why it was originally brought into the house.

The first allusions to any of these skulls appear at the end of the eighteenth century, but only as isolated cases. As antiquarians and folklorists exchanged information in the nineteenth century through such journals as the

Gentleman's Magazine and *Notes and Queries*, they realized that the pattern was a recurrent one. More and more examples came to light, for the topic appealed not only to folklorists but to investigators of the paranormal and compilers of popular collections of ghost lore; by the end of the twentieth century over two dozen cases were known, with at least ten skulls still in existence. At some point, apparently in late Victorian times, somebody coined the term 'Screaming Skull' with reference to the specimen at Bettiscombe Manor, although the earliest records do not specify screams as part of the ghostly manifestations there. This alliterative and melodramatic term is now the standard one.

The traditional legends told to account for these macabre objects often stress that it was at the dead person's own request that his or her skull was brought to the house, or that justice required that it be kept there. This reflects a natural horror at seeing human remains kept in unorthodox places rather than given seemly burial; it is assumed that nothing less than a powerful supernatural influence could justify such a shocking state of affairs. But why should anyone have made such a strange request? Each locality has evolved its own explanatory tale or tales; some tell of murders, others of the link binding the dead person to a family home. One of the best known is attached to Burton Agnes Hall, Yorkshire, and stresses a dead woman's passionate wish to remain in the house which she and her sisters were building, but which she did not live to see. At Tunstead Farm, Derbyshire, the famous guardian skull, 'Dickie', is supposed to have been the rightful owner of the farm, treacherously murdered.

The real history of these skulls cannot now be discovered. One prosaic suggestion is that some of them could be prehistoric specimens dug up by amateur archaeologists from local burial mounds, and preserved as curios. This would fit the Bettiscombe skull quite plausibly, because Pilsdon Pen, a hill overlooking the manor, is topped by Iron Age earthworks which may have included a ritual enclosure, with a spring of mineral waters nearby. This skull has a brownish patina consistent with having lain in mineral water for some long period, but it has not been carbon-dated. Other skulls may have belonged to medical students or artists, or been kept as a *memento mori* – a focus for meditation on death. In one case, at Wardley Hall, Lancashire, the skull is very probably that of a martyred Catholic priest, reverently preserved – but with a cover story to disguise the Catholic sympathies of the household.

Whatever their origin, these house skulls are now firmly situated in a framework of supernatural belief. Clearly, their function as family luck-bringers is identical to that of heirlooms such as the Luck of Edenhall, Cumberland. The Bettiscombe skull was said to ensure that no ghost could ever invade the house, which is reminiscent of the animal bones sometimes found hidden under floors or bricked up in chimneys and walls in old houses, probably as secret protections against witchcraft and other evil forces. The human skulls, however, were openly displayed, not hidden. In this, they resemble the carved heads and faces found on buildings of many periods, both religious and secular, which were sometimes thought to bring luck as well as being decorative.

One speculation, supported by Roberts and Clarke, suggests that the display of skulls and carved heads is an unwitting continuation of pre-Christian Celtic cult in which severed heads symbolized power, wisdom, and protection; this provides a good functional match, but involves a time lag of at least 1,500 years. Moreover, the existence of the Celtic head cult, strongly advocated by the archaeologist Ann Ross from the 1960s onwards, has more recently been questioned by the historian Ronald Hutton.

Spring-Heeled Jack

Spring-Heeled Jack, a figure in the popular imagination of the nineteenth and early twentieth centuries, is characterized by his ability to leap over high walls or across wide spaces, supposedly because of compressed springs in his boots.

Rumours about this figure (as yet nameless) swept through London and surrounding villages in the autumn and winter of 1837–8. On 8 January 1838, someone in Peckham anonymously warned the Lord Mayor of London that some men of high rank had laid a bet with 'a mischievous and foolhardy companion', challenging him:

[to visit] many of the villages near London in three different disguises – a ghost, a bear, and a devil; and, moreover . . . enter a gentleman's gardens for the purpose of alarming the inmates of the house. The wager has, however, been accepted, and the unmanly villain has succeeded in depriving seven ladies of their senses . . .

The affair has now been going on for some time, and, strange to say, the papers are still silent on the subject. The writer . . . has reason to believe that they have the whole history at their finger ends, but, through interested motives, are induced to remain silent.

The Times, 9 January 1838

According to the *Morning Chronicle* and the *Morning Herald*, the rumours had begun in Barnes the previous September; some forty villages and suburbs had been gripped by panic. The attacker was generally described as 'an unearthly warrior' in brass or steel armour, 'with spring shoes and large claw gloves', but occasionally as a white bear. Journalists tried to find witnesses, but failed:

A reporter . . . visited many of the places above mentioned, where he found that, although the stories were in everyone's mouth, no person who had actually seen the ghost could be found. He was directed to many persons who were named as having been injured by this alleged ghost, but, on his speaking to them, they immediately denied all knowledge of it, but directed him to other persons whom they had heard had been ill-treated, but with them he met with no better success; and the police . . . declare that, although they have made every enquiry into the matter, they cannot find one individual hardy enough to assert a personal knowledge on the subject.

Morning Herald, 10 January 1838

As further complaints poured in, vigilantes and police patrols were set up and rewards offered, but nobody was caught. Journalists christened the villain 'Spring-Heeled Jack'; they viewed him as a human prankster, but many people described him as a demon. The fullest picture was given by a girl called Jane Alsop, who on 20 February opened the door of her home in Bearbinder Lane, Bow, to a man claiming to be a police officer. He asked her for a candle, then vomited blue and white flames and attacked her, tearing at her dress and hair with what felt like metallic claws. She told Lambeth magistrates that he was wearing a large helmet and a tight-fitting white costume like an oilskin; his eyes were like balls of fire. Two or three men were interrogated, but released without charge (*The Times*, 22 February, 2 and 3 March 1838). On 28 February, another young girl, Lucy Scales from Limehouse, was found in hysterics in the street, saying she had been pounced on by a tall, cloaked man who spurted blue flames at her (*Morning Post*, 7 March 1838). She had just been reading a press account of the attack on Jane Alsop.

The London panic gradually died down, but others broke out in various towns over the next thirty or forty years, and were reported by various contributors to a correspondence in *Notes and Queries* in 1907. In Yarmouth in 1845, a delirious man wandering about in his nightshirt was mistaken for Spring-Heeled Jack and beaten up. In Peckham in 1872, there was alarm over a ghost leaping over walls and ditches, and vanishing with startling speed. In Sheffield in May 1873, rumours sprang up that a tall man in a sheet was scaring women for a bet; a mob searched the cemetery where he supposedly lurked, but found nobody, and clashed with the police. In 1877, at Aldershot barracks, two spectral figures 'glowing with phosphorus' and 'making tremendous springs of ten or twelve yards at a time' terrified the sentries. The last documented panics were at Liverpool in 1904 and in Bradford in 1926.

Spring-Heeled Jack entered fiction. In the 1840s, he figured in two plays (by J. T. Haines and by W. G. Wills) and an anonymous weekly 'penny dreadful'; in all three, he is an evil character. But another penny dreadful in the 1870s, probably written by George A. Sala, radically reshaped the legend. Sala's Jack, like today's Batman or Superman, uses his power to defeat the wicked; he is a nobleman by birth, though cheated of his inheritance. He wears a skintight crimson suit, with bat's wings, a lion's mane, horns, talons, massive cloven hoofs, and a sulphurous breath; he is immensely strong, and moves in gigantic leaps, thanks to his boots with their hidden springs.

St George

St George is thought to have been martyred in AD 303 at Lydda (Palestine), where his supposed tomb attracted pilgrims by the early sixth century; for several centuries he was little known in Western Europe, though revered in Byzantium for bringing victory in battle. His fame spread when Crusaders at the siege of Antioch (1098) saw heavenly warriors on white horses, led by the soldier saints George, Mercurius, and Demetrius, hurling spears at the Muslims – a vision described in the *Gesta Francorum* and by various twelfth-century chroniclers. A military and aristocratic cult rapidly developed, and was introduced into England by Richard the Lionheart. St George's feast day (23 April) was made a holiday in 1222; Edward III made him the patron of the Order of the Garter in the 1340s; Henry V invoked him at Agincourt; by the close of the Middle Ages he had replaced St Edward the Confessor and St Edmund of East Anglia as the patron saint of England.

Greek and Latin accounts of his life stress his appalling martyrdom – lasting seven years, in some versions. Three times he actually died, but each time God restored him to life to suffer further. Among other things, he was cut into ten pieces, beaten with iron rods, forced to drink molten lead, poisoned, sawn in half, and broken on a wheel, before being finally beheaded. His sufferings are shown in sixteenth-century windows in the church of St Neot, Cornwall.

His most famous exploit, his dragon combat, is first mentioned centuries later in *The Golden Legend*, a late thirteenth-century Latin collection of saints' lives by Jacobus de Voragine. It tells how George came to a pagan city where people had to sacrifice a girl's life every day to feed a dragon from a nearby lake, and the lot had fallen on the king's daughter; George wounded the monster, bound it with the princess's girdle, and led it into the city 'like a little dog upon a leash' before beheading it; the king and all his people became Christians. This is an allegory of a true Christian defeating the Devil, but it also has a strong appeal simply as an adventure. The people of Brinsop claimed it had happened in their village.

There was another, popular legend about St George in medieval England which appears in a versified charm in a manuscript dating from between 1420 and 1450, for protecting horses from witchcraft. It was commonly thought, well into the nineteenth century, that if a horse was tired and sweating in the morning, a witch or a fairy had been riding it during the night; to prevent this, one should hang a holed flint in the stable. The medieval charm says the stone should be hung at the stable door or over the horse's stall, together with a written verse:

> Seynt lorge, our ladys knyght,
> He walked day, he walked nyght,
> Till that he fownde that fowle wyght [foul creature];
> And when he her fownde,

> He her beat and her bownde,
> Till trewly ther her trowthe sche plyght [gave her word]
> That sche sholde not come be nyght
> With-inne vij rode [seven rods] of londe space
> Ther as Seynt leorge i-namyd was.

> In nomine Patri &c.

This implies that George once overcame a supernatural hag or witch, and banished her. About a century later, Thomas Blundeville (1564) quotes virtually the same rhyme, both for horses and for humans who are hagridden by the Nightmare – though he himself dismisses it as a 'fonde foolish charme'.

The legend of St George was too patriotic to be suppressed at the Reformation, but had to be remodelled to suit the Protestant ethos. This was done by Richard Johnson in 1596 in a popular work, *The Famous Historie of the Seven Champions of Christendom*, which strips out Christian elements, replacing them with chivalric and magical adventures imitated from medieval romances. In this version, George is born in Coventry to noble English parents, but stolen soon after birth by an enchantress whose power he eventually outwits. He saves Sabra, the King of Egypt's daughter, from a dragon, and has many further adventures; eventually he encounters a second dragon (on Dunsmore Heath, Warwickshire) and kills it, but dies from its poison, and is buried in Windsor chapel.

This version proved immensely popular, and ensured George's status in Protestant England. It also left its mark on the Mummers' Play, a comic folk drama performed in many parts of the country, usually at Christmas or Easter, apparently dating from the early eighteenth century. It consists of a series of single combats between its hero, generally called George ('king', not 'saint'), and various opponents called Bold Slasher, Turkish Knight, and the like. Either George or one of his enemies is killed, and revived by a comic doctor. Contrary to what some past scholars have claimed, the dragon hardly ever appears, but on his first entry the hero often boasts of this, the most enduring feature in his legend.

Stone Circles

Where standing stones occur, either singly or in groups, in an area not otherwise rocky, there will commonly be some legend to explain how they came to be there, or what strange powers they have. A solitary stone is usually said to have been thrown or dropped by the Devil, or a giant, or a mighty hero; a number of stones arranged in a circle, or in straight alignments, calls for more elaborate explanation.

In most cases, the traditional story asserts that the stones were living people, petrified because of their wickedness. The nature of their evil deed can vary. At Mitchell's Fold, Shropshire, a wicked old woman who milked a fairy cow dry was turned to stone, and other stones placed round her to pen her in. The Rollright Stones, Oxfordshire, are an invading king and his army, thwarted by fate and a witch's power. But in the majority of cases, the offenders are stricken by a divine punishment because they have broken the rules of Sunday observance, by working, or dancing, or playing some sport, on that holy day. One notable example is near Linkinhorne on Bodmin Moor, Cornwall, where three stone circles are collectively known as The Hurlers, and are said to have been men playing the characteristic Cornish ball game of 'hurling' on a Sunday afternoon. But dancing is the most common offence; to Christian moralists, both Catholic and Protestant, it was suspect because it encouraged sexual attraction, and became yet more wicked if it diverted people from their religious duties. It is also relevant that throughout the medieval period people danced in a ring, so the visual analogy with a stone circle was striking.

Stanton Drew, Somerset, a complex grouping of stone circles and avenues, is of especial interest because its legend has been repeatedly recorded over the last 340 years. The first to mention it was the antiquarian and archaeologist John Aubrey, who was attempting to make a plan of the monument in 1664; it was locally known as 'The Wedding', he wrote, because of a tradition concerning 'a bride going to be married' in which 'she and the rest of the company were metamorphosed into these stones.' A fuller version was given by William Stukeley in 1723; he says the wedding was on a Sunday, and links individual actors in the tragedy with specific stones: two in the centre are the bride and groom, those in the circle are the dancing guests, and two or three outliers 'sunk into a ditch' are the fiddlers. In a later description, of 1743, he also identifies the parson.

Another antiquarian, John Wood, in 1749, adds a sinister detail about the power of the stones themselves, which has parallels at Stonehenge, Wiltshire, and Aylesford, Kent:

No one, say the Country People about Stantondrue, was ever able to reckon the number of these metamorphosed Stones, or to take a Draught [sketch] of them, tho' several have attempted to do both, and proceeded till they were either struck dead upon the Spot, or with such an Illness as soon carried them off.

Writers of the nineteenth and twentieth centuries have generally said explicitly that the wedding was held on a Saturday, and that the dancing went on so late into the night that it overlapped into the Sunday, thus calling down God's wrath. It is probable that this scenario had been implicit from the first, for parallels both in Britain and abroad show that petrifaction is regularly associated with sacrilegious disrespect towards a sacred place, time, or object. In Protestant England, the clergy struggled to repress Sabbath-breaking, and the Stanton Drew story reflects this concern. In some versions, it is said that the fiddler (or piper), knowing midnight had come, refused to play on a Sunday and ran off; but the revellers swore they would carry on dancing, even if the Devil himself came to play for them. Which he did, slowly at first, but then faster and faster, and the dancers found they could not stop. Screams were heard, and by morning every living person had vanished, and the stones had appeared – some say, in the places where the dead dancers' bones lay. In these versions the musician survives, because of his piety; other storytellers apparently did not agree, for the monument has the alternative traditional name of The Fiddler and the Maids, which would indicate that he too, like Stukeley's musicians, shared in the guilt and in the doom.

The idea that those who offend God, or the gods, are turned to stone is deep-rooted: it occurs in the Bible as the punishment of Lot's wife (Genesis 19:26), and in various classical myths such as that of Niobe and her children. The particular form involving dancers can be traced back to a famous German religious tale from the early Middle Ages, first mentioned by the monk Lambert of Hersfield in 1075. He claimed that some sixty years previously, a group of peasants who were dancing in the churchyard at Kolbeck (Kölbigk, Germany) one Christmas Eve refused to stop when rebuked by the priest, who told them the Midnight Mass was about to start and they ought to attend it. They were cursed by the priest, so that they had to dance in the same place for a whole year without stopping, at the end of which time most of them fell dead. Later writers added that a ring of stones had been set up to mark the spot. The story spread throughout Europe and was often transferred to local sites, developing various new features.

Treacle Mines

Throughout Britain one finds villages which are jokingly said to possess a secret treacle mine; there are at least thirty of them. They may also have other imaginary industries such as jam butty mines or porridge quarries. The joke can be used in many different ways: sometimes it implies that people there are daft enough to think you can get treacle out of the ground by digging for it; sometimes, that they are so poor they live on bread and treacle only; sometimes, that they are lazy scroungers who go through life getting something for nothing; sometimes, that treacle-mining is a secret and highly profitable craft, unknown to outsiders. Since the implications are so varied, the joke can be used as a taunt by outsiders against villagers, but also (more frequently) by insiders as a mark of pride in their identity; a pub, or a football team, may be named after the mine. Local people can get a good deal of amusement out of persuading children, or gullible strangers, that treacle mines really exist, and often devise complicated stories to back up their hoax.

Thus at Chobham, Surrey, since the early twentieth century, if not longer, children have regularly assured one another that somewhere on the common one would find treacle mines. Some believed it; others were simply out to fool those younger than themselves into wasting time on a wild goose chase, until they realized at last that it was merely a leg-pull. There was a brisk exchange of letters on the topic in the *West Sussex Gazette* in 1973. A Mr David Fowler wrote that he had been told by a Chobham resident in 1961 that the existence of the mines was due to military waste and incompetence. He was told that when American (or Canadian) troops went home in 1919 they left behind a buried stockpile of supplies, including drums of treacle or syrup; these became totally corroded, owing to the acidity of the local Bagshot Sand, so that when someone accidentally dug into them they burst, creating the wondrous mines.

However, a letter-writer in the *Daily Mail* in January 1995 claimed that the Chobham mine dates back to 1853 and the start of the Crimean War, when over 8,000 soldiers encamped on the common for eight weeks before being reviewed by Queen Victoria and eventually embarking. Their supplies, which had been stored underground, were forgotten; these included thirty hogsheads of molasses, each containing 56 gallons. In 1901, they burst and flowed down the hill, leading the people of Woking to think they had discovered a natural source of treacle. During the First World War, the output of the mines was used to make sticky bombs and limpet mines, though only in winter; treacle was also poured into vacated trenches by the War Office to make them untenable if taken over.

A Mrs Austen, writing to the *West Sussex Gazette* on 12 July 1973, explained how she and her husband used to tell their children in the 1950s that a certain building at Patcham in Sussex (which in reality was a disused waterworks) housed the famed treacle mines which had given employment to local men for generations, and whose treacle was still much in demand. She would tell them how the mines were formed:

Millions of years ago, when England was a tropical country, before the Ice Age, sugar cane grew here. Year after year it grew, ripened and rotted unharvested, the molasses draining away down into the folds of the hills, where it accumulated above an impermeable layer of clay. The centuries passed, the colder weather came, and sugar cane no longer grew on the Downs, but the underground layer of treacle lay patiently waiting until in 1871 Peter Jones, a scientist who had long suspected its existence, sank the first shaft. The ensuing treacle gusher spouted for three days, covering the countryside for several miles around with a fine rain of treacle, until it was at last brought under control.

An underground lake of treacle also exists at Wareside, Hertfordshire, according to a letter-writer in the *Hertfordshire Mercury* in 2001:

I am writing to voice my concern at Wareside being a potential quarry site . . . Wareside is situated on a rich subterranean field of treacle, which is an extremely rare phenomenon. The treacle fields have lain dormant for many years now as they became economically unviable, but in their heyday they provided much-needed employment for local workers. My grandfather worked in the mines for many years and told me of the thriving black market trade where treacle was smuggled out in lunchboxes and sold to Mrs Widdy Waddy, who made treacle toffee in Red Lion Lane.

Should mining begin again in Wareside to extract sand and gravel, it may become extremely dangerous to local people if a dormant access shaft or long-forgotten treacle field is disturbed, as this may cause a huge spout of treacle which could envelop houses and fields.

Natland in the Lake District has a more romantic tale, according to Peter Walker's collection of local stories (1993). In the year 1211, a man searching for Roman treasures in a cavern saw an ancient pot apparently filled with gold, guarded by a snake. Recklessly he seized it; the snake bit him, his hand began to swell and throb, and he fainted, breaking the pot. But what it held was a golden syrup, which cured his hand at once. Knowing that this was more precious than any coins, the man explored the cave and found a spring of treacle. For centuries now this has brought health and wealth to the villagers, but no outsider is ever told where the golden spring may be.

The Undead

This modern term refers to a corpse that leaves its grave, with malevolent intent. If the grave is opened, the body will appear to have moved, or to be swollen, with a dusky or ruddy face, and full of blood – macabre effects which are in fact a stage of natural decomposition. It then has to be physically destroyed. There are very few traces of this belief in Britain's own traditions (although the East European vampire is familiar in recent popular culture) but some are found in the writings of William of Newburgh, a canon in the Augustinian priory at Newbury in Yorkshire. In 1197, he recorded four contemporary accounts of physically active corpses.

In 1196, says William, a dead man in Buckinghamshire entered the bed where his wife was sleeping, almost crushing her with his weight. The same happened next night, but on the third he was driven away by some friends she had asked to keep watch in her room. He then harassed his brothers, until they too drove him off, after which he caused panic among the farm animals. No one dared sleep at night, and some even saw him wandering abroad in the daytime.

At length the people appealed to their archdeacon for help, and he in turn consulted the Bishop of Lincoln. The bishop's advisors told him there would be no peace till the body was dug up and burnt. He rejected this as unseemly; instead, he wrote a letter of absolution, and ordered the tomb to be opened and the body examined. This was done and, since the corpse showed no unnatural changes in appearance, the pardon was put on its breast, after which it never wandered again.

At about the same time a similar thing happened in Berwick – 'by the contrivance of Satan', says William. A certain rich but evil man would come out of the grave at night and wander about till daybreak, pursued by a pack of barking dogs. Some townsfolk feared it would physically assault them, others that it would infect the air with disease. So they hired men to dig up the carcass, cut it limb from limb, and burn it.

William's third tale comes from a monastery at Melrose early in the 1190s. A certain dead friar, a pleasure-loving man who had been chaplain to the household of a noble lady, would leave his grave every night and haunt her bedchamber, groaning and muttering. In terror, she begged the friars to help, so two of them, together with two sturdy laymen, kept watch in the cemetery. At one point, when only one friar was on guard, his companions having gone indoors to warm themselves, the Devil caused the corpse to rise from its grave and rush at him with a fearful roar, so he drove an axe into it. It fled, groaning loudly; the friar chased it back to its tomb, which opened of its own accord for it to enter, and at once closed again. Next morning the four men together dug up the corpse, which had bled heavily. They carried it outside the monastery walls, burnt it, and scattered the ashes to the winds.

The fourth tale comes from a castle which William

calls Anantis; he may mean Alnwick in Northumberland, or possibly Annand in Dumfriesshire. A wicked man injured himself severely in a fall while jealously spying on his wife and her lover; as he lay dying, a priest urged him to repent and receive the Eucharist, but being still angry he refused, and died unshriven. Even so, he was given Christian burial, but every night he roamed about, pursued by barking dogs; people dared not go outside before dawn, for fear of meeting him and being beaten black and blue. Worse, his plague-ridden breath filled every house with disease and death. While the priest and others were debating what could be done, two young men decided to take matters into their own hands by destroying the corpse. They found it only lightly covered with earth; it was hugely bloated, its face suffused with blood, its shroud torn to shreds. When the spade struck it, it gushed blood like a leech. They smashed its side open with the spade, and tore the heart to pieces before throwing the body onto a fire. The plague then ceased.

Witches

In most folkloric contexts, a 'witch' is someone who uses magic to harm human beings, farm animals, or property. It is almost always a woman, and it is generally stated or implied that her power comes from the Devil.

Witchcraft was first declared a crime in English law in 1542, with hanging the penalty if human death had occurred, and imprisonment, fines, or the pillory for lesser injuries. Prosecutions were intermittent. Trials peaked in the 1580s and again in the 1640s, but declined sharply after 1660; the Witchcraft Acts were repealed in 1736, and the crime officially ceased to exist. But fear of suspected witches remained common for generations; there were even occasional incidents of mob violence against them in the nineteenth century. Protective charms and curative counter-spells were widely used.

These practical everyday fears and precautions were reflected in numerous personal anecdotes about misfortunes attributed to bewitchment, and steps taken to counteract it – such as this from an Oxfordshire village, reported by Angelina Parker in 1913:

An old lady once told me that, many years before, she was in a low, depressed state of mind, and her brother came to see her. He said solemnly, Jane, you're bewitched. I'll tell you what I will do. I will pin a cross over your door, and then no unholy thing can enter in.' He then placed two straws in the shape of a cross over the doorway. She did recover, but whether in consequence of the cross or not she could not say.

There were also more elaborate legends following stereotyped patterns, very common throughout Britain. The most widespread concerns a witch who turns into a hare; no hunter can catch or shoot it, and it runs towards her cottage. At length, one hound contrives to bite it in the hind leg or rump, or the huntsman wounds it with a silver bullet; in either case, the hare disappears into the cottage, where the old woman is found, bleeding from an identical wound. This story has been recorded in virtually every rural area; there is also a less common variation where the witch becomes a cat. Both are merely the British sub-types of an ancient and international theme. However, the belief that witches kept animal familiars is peculiar to England; these could be toads, as at Broomfield, Somerset, or mice, or cats.

In a legend from the Kennet Valley, Berkshire, the witch transforms another person, not herself. A farmer's wife uses a magic bridle to turn a farmhand into a horse and ride him to a witches' feast, till another man outwits and unmasks her, and she is put to death. This type of story was seriously used as evidence in three seventeenth-century trials: at Pendle Forest, Lancashire, in 1633; at Longstanton, Cambridgeshire, in 1659; and in 1673 in Northumberland, where a girl called Anne Armstrong said that a woman came to her as she lay in a fit and slipped a bridle over her head, riding her cross-legged till they came to a certain mill, where witches danced with a tall black man, feasted on food pulled from ropes, and danced in animal form.

Stories illustrating witches' power over animals were widespread, especially ones about bringing horses to an unexplained halt. To do this they might become straws, as at Wooton Basset, Wiltshire, or appear in person. The accounts from Billericay and Thundersley in Essex illustrate this, and also the beliefs that drawing a witch's blood would break her power, and that a physical attack on the bewitched object would somehow affect the witch herself. Other magical themes include the witch's ability to curse, to cast the evil eye, to send her familiars to harm someone, to ride across country on a hurdle or (more rarely) a broomstick, to hinder the churning of butter, to afflict someone with lice, and to cross rivers on a plank or in a tub (for example at Canewdon, Essex, and Newbury, Berkshire).

Alongside supernatural anecdotes are others embodying memories of actual individuals such as Hannah Henley, who died at Membury, Devon, in 1842, and possibly Mother Red Cap at Camden Town, London. An important factor in spreading and prolonging the fear of witches was the publicity surrounding major trials such as those at Warboys, Huntingdonshire and Peterborough, through pamphlets which circulated widely.

THE STORY OF PENGUIN CLASSICS

Before 1946 ...'Classics' are mainly the domain of academics and students, without readable editions for everyone else. This all changes when a little-known classicist, E. V. Rieu, presents Penguin founder Allen Lane with the translation of Homer's Odyssey that he has been working on and reading to his wife Nelly in his spare time.

1946 The Odyssey becomes the first Penguin Classic published, and promptly sells three million copies. Suddenly, classic books are no longer for the privileged few.

1950s Rieu, now series editor, turns to professional writers for the best modern, readable translations, including Dorothy L. Sayers's *Inferno* and Robert Graves's *The Twelve Caesars*, which revives the salacious original.

1960s 1961 sees the arrival of the Penguin Modern Classics, showcasing the best twentieth-century writers from around the world. Rieu retires in 1964, hailing the Penguin Classics list as 'the greatest educative force of the 20th century'.

1970s A new generation of translators arrives to swell the Penguin Classics ranks, and the list grows to encompass more philosophy, religion, science, history and politics.

1980s The Penguin American Library joins the Classics stable, with titles such as *The Last of the Mohicans* safeguarded. Penguin Classics now offers the most comprehensive library of world literature available.

1990s Penguin Popular Classics are launched, offering readers budget editions of the greatest works of literature. Penguin Audiobooks brings the classics to a listening audience for the first time, and in 1999 the launch of the Penguin Classics website takes them online to an ever larger global readership.

The 21st Century Penguin Classics are rejacketed for the first time in nearly twenty years. This world famous series now consists of more than 1,300 titles, making the widest range of the best books ever written available to millions – and constantly redefining the meaning of what makes a 'classic'.

The Odyssey continues ...

The best books ever written

PENGUIN CLASSICS

SINCE 1946

Find out more at www.penguinclassics.com